Photo credit Oliver Clyde

About the Author

Gerald Dickens is a great-great-grandson of Charles Dickens and has been performing one-man stage shows based on the life and works of his ancestor for thirty years, undertaking major tours of both the UK and America each year. He first performed a dramatic reading of *A Christmas Carol* in 1993 and over the years has developed it into an internationally acclaimed theatrical performance. He lives in Abingdon with his wife and youngest children.

Gerald Dickens: My Life on the Road with A Christmas Carol

Gerald Dickens

Gerald Dickens: My Life on the Road with A Christmas Carol

Olympia Publishers
London

www.olympiapublishers.com
OLYMPIA PAPERBACK EDITION

Copyright © Gerald Dickens 2023
Cover Image: Martin Smith, Origin8 Photography

A CIP catalogue record for this title is
available from the British Library.

ISBN: 978-1-80439-421-2

This is a work of creative nonfiction. The events are portrayed to the
best of the author's memory. While all the stories in this book are
true, some names and identifying details have been changed to
protect the privacy of the people involved.

First Published in 2023

Olympia Publishers
Tallis House
2 Tallis Street
London
EC4Y 0AB

Printed in Great Britain

Dedication

Dedicated to my wife Liz and my children Cameron, Lily and Layla. To my mother and father, David and Betty Dickens, and to my brother and sisters Liz, Ian and Nicky. To all of those friends and colleagues over the years who have helped to make my show what is today. Finally, to the audiences, without whom none of this would be possible.

Acknowledgements

With thanks: to Paul Standen, Caroline Jackson, Bob and Pam Byers.

This is a story of a life on the road. For over thirty years I have toured extensively in the USA sometimes in the footsteps of, often in the shadow of, my great-great-grandfather Charles Dickens who himself revelled in the opportunity to step upon a stage and charm audiences with his extraordinary theatrical skills. Over the years I have visited many places and made many friends and seen many sights. I have been incredibly fortunate to stay in some remarkable hotels, and to have driven through some breath-taking scenery and the memories I have will stay with me forever.

This book is my story about those memories, how I came to be an actor and how my performance of *A Christmas Carol* grew into what it is today.

Chapter 1
How Did It All Begin?

I was born in the county of Kent on the 9 October 1963, the forth and youngest child to David and Betty Dickens. We lived in Southborough, a small village which was enclosed within the larger town of Tunbridge Wells, nay, Royal Tunbridge Wells to give it its full regal title. Southborough confusingly lies to the north of Tunbridge Wells and is so called because it was originally attached to the much older town of Tonbridge. Today Tunbridge Wells has a reputation for tradition and stolidity, but the town is a relative newcomer in the history of the region. After the Norman Conquests of 1066 tracts of land were given to noblemen who had assisted in the fight against King Harold, and an area around the Medway Valley was gifted to Richard Fitz Gilbert who built a grand castle on the riverbank. The old English name comes from 'ton' meaning a manor, and obviously the 'bridge' across the River Medway. Fitz Gilbert's land spread wide and included The Manor of Southborough. Through the medieval times Southborough became independent from Tonbridge and eventually reverted to the Crown's ownership. King Henry VIII would gift it to Anne Boleyn's brother George (the Boleyn family lived at the nearby Hever Castle and Henry was a frequent visitor).

All of this history makes Southborough sound as if it is a very grand neighbourhood but today you would be hard pressed to find any sign of the glorious past, for it is just another community straddling another through road. In 1963 the Dickens family resided in a small bungalow in a quiet cul de sac, Bryan Crescent. The house must have been bursting at the seams already and with the addition of a fourth child my mother and father almost immediately realised that they would have to move to more spacious surroundings.

Dad was a publisher and each morning he would don his bowler hat and grasp his furled umbrella to join the army of similarly attired gentlemen who made their way into London. The area around Tunbridge Wells was perfectly situated for a commuter with superb rail links to Charing Cross in the very heart of the West End. Each weekday morning, he would leave (before we children were awake) and each evening he would return (often after we were asleep) – a most conservative and reliable and respectable existence, but there was so much more to Dad than that.

He was a countryman at heart and was never happier than when he was striding across the landscape wielding a walking stick, often hewn by his own hand, preferably clambering over barbed-wire fences bearing signs reading: KEEP OUT! NO ENTRY! PRIVATE PROPERTY! One of his favourite notices read 'Trespassers will be IMMIDIATELY prosecuted' and he would joke that if we went into that property, we would no doubt find a judge sitting in his wig and robes behind a desk waiting to pass sentence on us all.

Dad came from a Naval family and the Senior Service ran deep in his blood. His father, Gerald, had been an Admiral in the Royal Navy, and had been Knighted by King George VI on the deck of his ship at the Royal Naval Spithead Revue of 1937. All three of Gerald's sons, Peter, Claud and my father, David, had joined the Navy and it shaped their lives. Give Dad a length of rope and he would splice away as if nothing else in the world mattered. Camping holidays in Scotland were run along Naval lines, with each member of the family having their own duties – fetching fresh water from a stream, collecting firewood, or washing up dishes, but the most odious of tasks – emptying the bucket in the little green tent pitched at some distance to the rest of the camp (it was known as The Spanish Residence, or El San), was left to Dad.

A new member of the family meant that staying at 27 Bryan Crescent was impossible and my parents began to look for a new house. They very much wanted to stay in the area as my older siblings, Liz, Ian and Nicky, were well established at their school and the daily commute to London was extremely convenient, so the search centred on Tunbridge Wells. Soon the perfect house was found – it was a late Victorian property with three floors, and five bedrooms. It was very grand and even boasted a sort of conical tower at one corner and a balcony to the front. Fate seemed to be waving her hand over my parents in that the house was also number 27 as the home at Bryan Crescent in Southborough had been. There was only one problem, such a grand house in such a desirable town cost a great deal of money – money which Mum and Dad simply did not have, but a white knight came riding to their rescue in the unlikely shape of my aging grandmother Pearl. Gerald had died in 1962, just under a year before I was born, and his widow was looking for a home and company, so it was agreed that she would make up the shortfall in the purchase price and move into the upper story of the house which could be arranged as a self-contained flat. And so it was that before I was even a year old the Dickens family moved into 27 Boyne Park, my childhood home.

Life at Boyne Park was wonderful and as many of the neighbours were of similar ages we grew into a happy group of friends, playing in each other's houses and gardens. When it was time for me to start school my mother and father decided to send me to a brand-new establishment, Bishop's Down Primary School, at which I would be among the first wave of pupils. Many of my friends went there too as it was close by and convenient, so we formed quite a tight knit community. Bishop's Down was run along modern lines, embracing new theories of education, so that rather than constantly droning our times tables by rote we were taught in a different way (I can't for the life of me remember what system they used, but it didn't work for me because to this day I am hopeless at multiplication). When it came to learning to read and write, again a new theory was espoused – ITA. ITA, or the Initial Teaching Alphabet was a phonetic system, based on Latin and designed by Sir James Pitman. The fact that my father worked for Pitman Publishing and knew Sir James maybe explains why I was sent to a school that embraced ITA, rather than the more traditional establishment that my siblings had attended. If the intent had been to simplify learning, the system didn't seem to come up to mark as it was based on an incredibly complicated alphabet of hieroglyphs each of which represented a specific sound 'sh' 'th' 'aye' etc. There were forty-five different symbols, and whilst I have already admitted that my mathematical skills are not great, it seems to me that ITA had roughly double the characters of the standard alphabet.

ITA would eventually die out as an unsuccessful experiment, but what it, and Bishop's Down, did achieve was to give me an opportunity to experiment and explore and not be too rigidly tied down to convention, and that is an asset that has served me well throughout my professional life.

At Bishop's Down School
Photo Credit Author's Collection

The days at Boyne Park and Bishop's Down School seem endless to me now, Mum created magic in the kitchen cooking huge Sunday roasts, amazing dinners, and the most extraordinarily lavish picnics if we went on a family trip. Dad would spend his weekends in the garden getting his hands in the soil or taking us for long Sunday afternoon walks. He also loved to make things, often on a grand scale, and in 1969 he agreed to help the local branch of the RSPCA in creating a float for the Tunbridge Wells carnival and it was a project that he threw himself into with extreme enthusiasm. A usual carnival float may have been based on a flatbed lorry, decorated with some balloons and placards, with various people standing nervously on it as it lurched forward and shuddered to a stop again. Music would be played through speakers and a team of walkers would collect loose change from the crowd and maybe distribute sweets and treats to the children watching. This approach was far too conventional for my father and instead he decided that he would build a thirty-foot-long model of the Loch Ness Monster that would apparently glide along the route under its own power.

Through the Spring months of 69 the area to the rear of Boyne Park became a massive construction site as 'Nessie' took shape. She was built on a timber frame which then had chicken wire attached to it to form the shape of the body, and finally a skin of papier-mâché was laid over which could be painted. It was a remarkable beast with a long neck holding its head high, the three distinctive humps as seen in the many photographs of the 'real' beast from Loch Ness and a long serpentine tail. The humps were not only there for factual accuracy, but also allowed three hefty men room to stand inside (unseen by the crowd) to push the creature along. The whole thing was painted green and the flesh had a scaly appearance, created by hundreds of little cups cut from cardboard egg boxes. The face was kindly, and the eyes had huge flirtatious lashes.

During the build various problems or design faults would arise necessitating more timber or hardware to solve, and at such time my increasingly agitated father would bark at my mother to go and purchase more screws, or brackets, or casters, or whatever he may need. Our local hardware store, RN Carr, was a very old-fashioned shop which smelt of oil and compost, and the brown-coated shopkeeper grew increasingly bemused as Mrs Dickens continually appeared asking for bags of screws. Obviously, this woman had no idea what she was doing so the staff rather patronisingly asked her 'Maybe if you tell us what you are trying to achieve, we can help you buy what you want – what exactly is it that you are making?' My mother was never one to be patronised and fixed Mr Carr with a steely eye: 'A thirty foot long Loch Ness Monster on wheels.' One silenced shopkeeper, one satisfied mother!

Dad's creation was a huge success and won a rosette for 'Best Self-Propelled Float' in that year's carnival. I was five years old at the time and was dressed in a kilt and tweed jacket and shyly lead my pet monster through the streets of Tunbridge Wells.

A very shy little boy leading Nessie
Photo Credit: Author's Collection

27 Boyne Park was always a flamboyant place, but it was at Christmas when it shone at its brightest. Christmas was of course a huge event in the Dickens family, and to celebrate it well was in the blood. Dad went to extreme lengths to decorate, and on the Sunday before Christmas, we would gather holly boughs, ivy and huge branches of fir which we would then lay out on a large blanket in the hallway. Behind every picture hanging on the walls an arrangement of greenery was pushed, whilst the wooden banisters on the stairway had fir woven through the balusters like an ancient display of country hedge laying. The smell of greenery was sublime.

The Christmas tree was always too big for the room – Dad would carefully measure the height but when we got to the shop he would inevitably say 'No, that doesn't look nearly large enough, we will take a bigger one!' and back at the house gentle surgery had to be performed to squeeze the tree in to an old coopered wooden barrel and manoeuvre it into place beneath the high ceiling There was nothing subtle about the decorating of the tree either. There was no theme or colour scheme, it was simply a case of covering even tiny fragment of green with colour. Glass baubles hung, tinsel wound, strips of coloured foil dangled, and strings of lights twinkled – it was a magical sight.

On Christmas Eve there was often a large drinks party for friends and neighbours, and I was designated the important duty of taking bowls of nuts and nibbles around, no doubt helping myself to more than were taken by the guests. And then there was Snap Dragon, this was an adult way of eating almonds and raisins, for they were soaked in a dish of brandy and then set alight. Because the burning point of alcohol is relatively low it was possible to plunge your fingers into the flames and pull out a handful of now roasted almonds and fruit

20

without injuring yourself and your fingers would apparently be burning with a blue flame. It all seemed very dangerous at the time, but it elicited gales of laughter and merriment which filled those old walls.

Christmas Day itself had a never changing routine: overnight our stockings which we had left hanging at the end of the beds had magically been filled. There were standard items that Father Christmas brought every year – a tangerine in the toe, some nuts, and a Christmas cracker, but then there would be the other presents such as masks and puzzles, pencil sharpeners and erasers, tricks and games all bulging out of the woollen socks that had seen service in the Navy and had been darned and repaired many times, but were now enjoying their retirement, bringing joy and wonder to the children of the house.

Of course, we woke early and emptied the stockings and began playing with the toys, but soon we would run downstairs to where the tree stood proudly protecting the mountain of wrapped presents that had appeared overnight, but we were not allowed to open them yet; that wasn't part of the day's timetable. Next was breakfast and the table in the dining room was already laid (what time Mum and Dad got to sleep or what time they woke I can't imagine). Fresh grapefruit, boiled eggs with cold ham (one year Mum tried to cure her own ham in brine, which wasn't a successful experiment!), followed by toast and marmalade – delicious.

Next was our traditional trip to Church. We were not a church-going family as a rule, but on Christmas morning it was essential that we dressed up smartly in our Sunday best and drove to St Peter's Church in Southborough. The service seemed interminably long to an excited child with unwrapped presents waiting under the tree, but it probably wasn't. We

21

attended a 'Family Service' which was geared towards children and at one point the vicar would invite children to bring up their favourite presents, this caused a degree of jealousy within me because it was apparent that other children had already unwrapped their 'big presents' whereas I had a pencil sharpener to show. I remember one year a boy brought a toy machine gun with him and the vicar, a preacher of peace on Earth, was momentarily silenced. 'Ah, how… nice' was all he managed to say.

When the Church service was done and we had all dutifully shaken hands and chatted with the vicar outside, as if we attended every week, we returned home with the excitement mounting. But still there was to be no present unwrapping, for the final preparations had to be made for lunch. Mum had put the gargantuan turkey in the oven early that morning whilst the pudding had been steaming away on the hob for just as long. The Christmas pudding, the highlight of our lunch, had been mixed and made during the summer and we all would have stirred the mixture having made a secret wish as we did it. When the mix was ready it was spooned into a bowl and covered with muslin cloth, then it was put away into a cool dark cupboard. In the early hours of Christmas morning the pudding bowl was placed in a pan of simmering water, and it was left to steam throughout the day (the muslin giving the kitchen the smell of 'a washing day' as Charles Dickens described in *A Christmas Carol*).

And now, as lunch approached, we could gather in the Drawing Room in front of the tree. Dad had lit a fire which crackled in the hearth and then prepared drinks for all that required them, the traditional adult tipple being a Horse's Neck – a drink with Royal Naval heritage being made from Brandy and Dry Ginger. And now, at last Dad would ask to be spun round (maybe blindfolded, I don't recall) so that there could be no favouritism in the choice of the first present given, he would carefully read the label: 'To Gerry, from Grandma' or whatever it may be. Soon the floor was awash with discarded wrapping paper and Mum tried in vain to keep track of where everything was and who it belonged to. Laughter, hugs and occasionally tears as genuine thanks were offered by everyone to everyone else. When the last of the presents had been handed out, the wrapping paper was thrown away (probably along with a vital set of instructions for a model or game), and we all posed for a traditional photograph, proudly displaying our spoils.

Glasses were recharged and the children investigated their new toys whilst the adults talked. Soon however, Mum disappeared back to the kitchen to continue to cast her magical spells over turkey, potatoes, sprouts, parsnips, pigs in blankets, gravy, stuffing, bread sauce, and goodness knows what else. We would feast well, whilst Dad constantly quoted *A Christmas Carol,* raising a glass to toast 'God Bless Us, Every One' and describe the turkey, 'It *was* a Turkey! He never could have stood upon his legs, that bird. He would have snapped 'em short off in a minute, like sticks of sealing wax.'

Second helpings were offered and devoured until eventually the dishes were cleared away and mum again disappeared into the kitchen, for it was now that she channelled her inner Mrs Cratchit as she dealt with the final stages of serving the Christmas Pudding that had been four months in the cooking. As we sat expectantly at the table, waiting for the pudding, Mum got to unwrap it and discover if it were at all edible – Mrs Cratchit's comical panic as to whether 'It should be done enough' or whether 'It should break in the turning out' was all too real for generations of British families.

Of course, it was fine, it was always perfect! Bowls of brandy butter were placed on the table as well as jugs of cream, and the curtains were closed. Now it was Dad's turn to take centre stage as he heated a small saucepan of brandy until the surface began to break, then he would put a match to it and WHUMMPH! Up went the blue flames. He poured the liquid fire over the pudding, making the sprig of holly stuck into the top sizzle and spit, and the order was given for the lights to be turned out. With all the theatricality of a true Dickens at Christmas Dad would parade the pudding around the table, aiming to complete the circuit before the flames died. It was perfect, and deep within the mix were lucky sixpenny pieces (Mum very carefully watching for them during the serving so that she could ensure everyone had one on their plate).

As if turkey with all of the trimmings followed by the densest, heaviest, richest pudding you could ever imagine were not enough, fruit and cheese and nuts, as well as mince pies, were then brought to the table and the banquet continued. Crackers were pulled, paper hats donned, and awful jokes told

At three o'clock in the afternoon the television (black and white) was brought in on a kitchen trolley and the mood became reverential as we listened to the words of our Queen who traditionally sent a Christmas message to the Commonwealth on Christmas afternoon. These days the contents of the Monarch's speech are often leaked beforehand, as is the case with so many public proclamations, but at that time it was as if the Queen was actually speaking to us live from Windsor Castle having just finished her own Christmas lunch, and we hung on her every word.

After the Queen had finished it was time for a walk, a chance to work off some of those calories, and we would look at the Christmas decorations that adorned the houses in our neighbourhood, passing judgement on the creativity and taste of the various efforts. When we got back to the house lunch had been tidied away and it somehow seemed appropriate to have some tea at which point Mum would place a huge Christmas cake in the centre of the table, with icing like a snow drift and model figures of Santa Clause, snowmen and reindeer stuck deep into it. As with the pudding this was a dense rich fruit cake, with nuts and cherries and raisins, and was absolutely delicious.

The day was waning fast now, and evening came upon us, Dad would stoke the fire so it roared once more and we would settle down as a family to watch the television – the Morecambe and Wise Christmas special was always on followed by a film of some kind, a James Bond or The Great Escape, neither of which seemed to quite embrace the Christmas spirit.

One Christmas, when I was still quite young, my Uncle Claud and Auntie Audrey accompanied by their children Kate and Rowland, came to stay with us and on that Christmas Eve Uncle Claud gathered us all in the largest bedroom, as if it were a dormitory, and read *A Christmas Carol* to us. This is my first memory of Charles Dickens' 'ghostly little book'. The volume he used was an edited version of the story that had been published by the Dickens Museum in London and was perfect for reading aloud. I remember being both astounded and confused at the end of the book when Scrooge realised that 'the spirits have done it all in one night!' How could that be so? The ghost of Jacob Marley had told us all that the first ghost would visit on one night, the second on the next and the third on the next after that – three days, and yet here was Ebenezer Scrooge awaking on Christmas morning, just a few hours after Marley's visit. This was a conjuring trick, a sleight of hand, a clever piece of misdirection by Charles Dickens who was indeed a keen amateur magician, although of course I didn't know that at the time.

I will never forget Claud's reading of the book and the effect it had on me. Today whenever I perform at Byers' Choice in Chalfont, Pennsylvania my cousin Rowland comes to see the show with his family, and we catch up on old times. Rowland now works in New York City and is hugely successful.

Back at Bishop's Down School there was no hint that my career was about to be formed, at that time my passion was for Formula One Grand Prix racing and as far as I was concerned, I was going to be a World Champion racing driver one day. I would make paper crash helmets decorated in my proposed racing colours and run around imaginary circuits emulating my heroes: Jackie Stewart, Emerson Fittipaldi, Graham Hill and Ronnie Peterson. There was a very brief flirtation with private investigation too when a fellow student fell on the playground and cut her head open, necessitating her being taken to hospital in an ambulance, which caused great excitement at the school. I felt that the circumstances behind this supposed 'accident' needed uncovering and quickly gathered a few friends around me to form Dickens Detectives. After a lot of interviewing and note taking (largely illegible I am sure) we discovered that our victim had been running on wet autumnal leaves made slippery by morning rain and slipped over. Verdict, accident, and so Dickens Detectives closed its only case.

During the same autumn term Bishop's Down School began to make arrangements for that year's Nativity play and it was the decisions made then that would change my life. As I have already mentioned, Bishop's Down was a very modern and forward-looking school and wanted to present that front to the parents and wider public. A traditional nativity play, with shepherds wearing tea-cloths on their heads, kings with card and foil crowns and angels with coat hanger and tinsel halos however charming would be at odds with the school's mission statement. So, discussions were had until eventually a whole new style of Nativity Play was proposed: why not tell the story through the eyes of the various animals in the stable? Mary and Joseph would be present, gathered around the manger, but they would remain largely silent, communicating their part of the story through the medium of mime.

We were all cast and began to learn our lines during a series of rehearsals, at least I assume that we did for I remember nothing about the build-up, my memory being dominated by later events.

As the weeks passed so Christmas got ever nearer and preparations continued, not least the making of costumes which endeavour was given over to the parents of the cast. Letters were sent to our respective homes, which read:

Bishop's Down School
Dear Mr and Mrs _____

We are very excited to let you know that your daughter/son has been cast in our Nativity Play and will be playing the part of a _____.

We would be very grateful if you please make a costume for her/him?

Yours sincerely

The letter that arrived at the Dickens household had 'daughter' crossed out and in the blank space was written the word 'Cockerel'. I am not sure that I have ever discovered if there actually was a cockerel in the Bethlehem stable, but for the purposes of the play one had been included in the drama and a costume would need to be created.

It so happened that my mother was away on business and therefore it was left to my father, with assistance from my older brother Ian, to make me a simple costume. The spirit of endeavour that had created Nessie a few years before was now re-awoken and Dad decided that there would be nothing simple about THIS costume. He and Ian got to work and whilst other children had their costumes made, I had mine built. Two large cardboard profiles of a cockerel were made and had to be braced with batons of timber to stop them flopping. Once the structure was made Ian got to work on the painting which he did with the hand of an artist (he would go on to study photography at art college), and a teenager of the psychedelic early seventies. The likes of this cockerel had never been seen in nature for its plumage was green and red and gold and blue. A huge red comb towered above the head and pendulous wattles wobbled beneath. And to create the effect of feathers the body sections were covered with brown paper shapes glued only at their top edge so that they would appear to flutter as I walked. The tail was a thing of wonder for it was made from ribbons, streamers and tinsel which glistened in the light.

When the construction was done, I was sandwiched in between the two halves and further batons of wood were screwed between them for me to hold as well as offering further bracing to the whole structure. I was quite a small, weakly child and I had trouble controlling this beast, so my dad reverted to his Naval days and fetched a length of rope to tie me in until the costume and I were as one.

When the day of the performance arrived, I couldn't change with the other children in our classroom (I wouldn't have been able to get out of the door), so Dad had to assist me

28

into the costume at the edge of the stage, meaning that nobody saw the full effect until my first entrance: The play started and the actors playing Mary and Joseph took their places at the front of the stage, but the first speaking character to enter was the donkey who had carried them to Bethlehem and was in need of rest. The donkey was played by a neighbour of ours and her costume was somewhat simpler than mine, for it consisted of nothing more than a leotard with a tail pinned on and maybe a small mask, or face paints. Out of curiosity a cow then entered the stable and engaged the donkey in polite conversation, enquiring who these people were that were settling down in the stable. The cow being the donkey's best friend in everyday life, their costumes were very similar in style and execution. "I must introduce you to my friends," said the cow, "and you can tell us what is happening in our stable. Cockerel, cockerel! Come here."

As I made my entrance it became apparent that in the original letter home no thought had been given to the relative scale of the animals, for as I blundered my way into the set there was a gasp from the audience, a shuffling and scraping as chairs were pushed backwards and then a nervous laughter at this apparently mutant rooster which towered over both cow and donkey. Inside my costume, I heard the laughter and it sounded good. I think that I knew in that moment that my future would be on the stage.

For a shy and insecure little boy, I had discovered a way of being confident and outgoing, if only for an hour or so on the stage. It was not that I didn't like being Gerald Dickens, it was just that I wished Gerald Dickens could be a little more exciting and interesting. By being someone else, or by inhabiting a different world for a short time, I could live an alternative existence and the benefits to my own personality were huge. This is a very common trait among actors: you may see us on the stage being larger than life and apparently extremely confident, but on the whole that shy insecure creature is very near the surface.

A few years ago, I worked as a front of house manager in a small theatre which was named in honour of one Britain's theatrical Knights, Sir Donald Sinden. During a long and hugely impressive career Sinden had played the great Shakespearean leads with the Royal Shakespeare Company as well as appearing in many films. To honour his eightieth birthday we invited him to the theatre to talk about his career and share some of his anecdotes from a lifetime treading the boards. The tickets sold out within a day of going on sale and The Sinden Theatre had never seen a crowd like it. The audience arrived early, and the excitement and anticipation were palpable. The loud ovation when Donald took to the stage in a bright orange jacket brought tears to many eyes. For the next two hours this amazing man electrified the theatre and had everyone in fits of laughter as he shared his memories, interspersed with some awful jokes (his favourite being set at the scene of an Olympic Games. For the purposes of the evening Donald cast himself into the joke and explained that he had seen a man walk past with a long aluminium pole over his shoulder. "Ah," said Donald, "are you a pole vaulter?" To which the fellow replied, 'Nein, I am German, but how did you know that my name was Walter?')

As the clock ticked towards our theatre's curfew Donald had only reached the year 1952, and the audience would have sat in that auditorium all night long, but we had to finish. When he took his bows the standing ovation, accompanied by stamping of feet and cheering, was extraordinary and the love for this gentle yet great man was clear. We brought a birthday cake onto the stage and the audience sung a rousing rendition

30

of 'Happy Birthday to You' and then there were more ovations and cheers. Eventually Donald left the stage and returned to his dressing room. After a suitable time, I knocked on his door to see if there was anything he needed, he said "come in" and there he sat, still in his orange jacket, he seemed to have shrunk and looked up at me with genuine concern in his eyes: 'Did they like it? Was I all right?' The insecure actor was ever present, even in such a successful man.

From discovering that I enjoyed performing (I think that the word 'acting' is too grand a description for those early efforts), I tried to get involved in any performance that I could and when I left Bishop's Down School and moved up to Huntleys Secondary school I began to act more and more. Huntleys was not a particularly artistic school, neither was it particularly academic, but it prepared its pupils for a life of work – metalwork, woodwork and technical drawing were all subjects that would lead boys towards apprenticeships. Boys were encouraged to follow their own paths, so it is no coincidence that an extraordinary number of pupils from Huntleys would go on to form their own businesses.

Theatre wasn't large on the curriculum and any performances relied very much on there being one teacher who was keen. My brother had attended Huntleys a few years before me and in his time a teacher by the name of Nigel Touch had galvanised a group of students to produce some extraordinary productions, including Macbeth. Mr Touch not only directed superb plays but also instilled a strong sense of discipline and professionalism into his casts, on one occasion berating them for presenting a thank you gift to him on stage after the last night of a run. 'You have ruined everything that we worked for, the audience will now go home thinking of us, instead of the characters in the play. You have broken the spell.

Never do that again!' Having said that, he was very grateful for his gift and touched that the boys should have made a collection in his honour.

In my day it was Anita Walker, an English teacher, who was keen on theatre and took it upon herself to put on plays. I quickly registered my interest (rehearsals often coincided with rugby training which I was quite happy to miss), and soon I was being cast in lead roles. One year we staged a play called A Penny for a Song, which was set in the grounds of a Dorset mansion and featured an eccentric landowner called Sir Timothy Bellboys who wanted to protect Britain from Napoleon's invasion by galvanising his staff into a private army. I was cast as a rather bumbling servant called Humpage who spent the entire show sat in a dinghy up a tree (he was the squire's lookout), and in answer to repeated enquiries as to whether the enemy were approaching, he simply answered 'No Zurr!' and in answer to enquiries as to whether he had a clear field of vision and was being vigilant on his watch, he simply answered 'Yes Zurr!' It was not a major role and certainly didn't move the plot forward at all, but a reporter from the local newspaper was suitably impressed by my efforts. Having written about the principal actors he then moved on to my performance, and wrote:

'And no major criticism of these three fine performances is implied when I say they were slightly 'upstaged' by their supporting cast – particularly Gerald Dickens as the satly sailor lookout Humpage.'

'It was an excellent and detailed performance for which he deserves great credit. Marooned in a land-locked boat – a crow's nest in the fanatical Bellboy's garden – Humpage had the twin handicaps of only a few lines to say and a broad west country accent in which to say them. But Gerald overcame his character's handicaps with some telling and revealing 'character' looks which held his audience's attention, even when the action itself ignored him.'

Reading between the lines I was obviously massively over-acting and a life as a solo performer clearly beckoned!

I won that year's drama cup at the school and again the following year – in fact for a while nobody else won it because I was the only one in the school who focussed solely on drama. There were plenty of other performers of course, but they had other interests besides, and mostly saw plays as a good way of meeting girls, whereas I would stay at the school late into the night helping to build and paint the sets, as well as concentrating on my own roles. I was riding high and began to get very cocky and arrogant but was soon brought crashing back to earth in a very public manner.

We were staging a production of Hans Christian Andersen's The Tinder Box, and I had been cast as the King, which seemed entirely appropriate to me. At one point during the performance, I was on stage alone, sat on my throne. Another character had been present at a royal audience and had just exited leaving me to make my next speech, and I froze, I couldn't remember my line. There is absolutely no excuse for this, for even if the actual line momentarily goes, an actor should know the script well enough to be able to say something, anything, to keep the plot moving on. On that occasion I hadn't learned the entire script well enough and wasn't prepared. As I sat on the stage nothing came to me and I felt completely exposed. Fortunately, we had a prompter sitting in the wings, a teacher, and now I relied on her to save me. When it became apparent that I was not pausing for dramatic effect the prompter, a rather timid lady, whispered my line so that the audience would not hear her, unfortunately I couldn't hear what she said either. Remaining in character I rose from my throne and with a regal flourish made my way to the side of the stage where she sat, and again she whispered the line, but still I could not hear. I hissed to her 'louder'. Now she shouted the line so loudly that not only I, but the entire audience could hear it: 'I AM LOST FOR WORDS!' The howl of laughter that followed was so humiliating that it haunts me still and I vowed never to be so poorly prepared again, and that is something that has served me well during my career as a one-man performer.

It was while I was at Huntley's school that a friend of mine mentioned a drama club that he went to once a week, called Design Theatre Workshop, or DTW for short, and wondered if I would like to try a few sessions. DTW had been formed a few years before and didn't exist purely to put on shows, but to explore ways of becoming more creative. The 'workshop' aspect saw us spend many evenings doing various improvisations and exercises, developing ways of creating our own theatre. I remember that one session was given over purely to feeling the strength of a gesture all the way through the arm to the very tip of the finger, every muscle tensed to create the desired effect and that is a technique that I use in my performance of *A Christmas Carol* today to bring strength and power to the Ghost of Christmas Yet to Come.

When it came to actual shows DTW produced some amazing theatre – we were a youth group and everything was done from within; no expert adult assistance. There was a seniority within the club with two Pauls, Low and Standen, running things and directing and a superb set designer, Steve, who provided the background for our efforts. Sound, lighting, stage management, publicity, sponsorship-finding was all undertaken by school kids, aged from eleven upwards, and we produced some magic.

In the early years I acted, the first production I can recall being involved with was Nikolai Gogol's The Government Inspector, and I think it was during a rehearsal for this production that my father, who will regularly appear at important moments throughout this story, once again assisted me in my future career. My great problem in those days was that I used to speak too quickly, to gabble, so that the carefully crafted dialogue was inaudible to an audience. After the experience of The Tinder Box, I was so scared of forgetting my lines that I would rush through every speech as rapidly as possible, fearing that a pause would lead to that dreaded silence again, and I never wanted to be back in that dark place.

During rehearsals for The Government Inspector Paul Low, the director, would tell me at every meeting, 'Gerald, you have to slow down, we can't hear your lines!' Dad would come and pick me up from the rehearsals and would often be standing in the hall when Paul gave his closing notes and obviously became a bit concerned that the same thing was said every week and I didn't seem to be capable of changing what I was doing. So, one week, when we were in the car, he addressed the issue with me: 'Every week you are asked to slow down and yet you never do, what is happening?' I explained as well as I could that I was trying to do what Paul said but didn't seem able to control my pace. Dad thought for a while and then came out with an extraordinary statement that transcended anything that I could have learned in drama school, he said, "Always finish one word before you begin the next one". It may have been, "Never start one word until you have finished the one before" but the meaning was the same and it was brilliant in its simplicity, it is a technique I still use to this day.

The DTW years were amazing, and I learned so much

about all aspects of the theatre. If I wasn't cast in a production, I made sure that I was involved some other way and therefore realised how much every aspect came together to create a production. As time went on, I began to direct too and that gave me an indication as to how an entire production actually looked from the back of a hall, whereas as an actor I'd only selfishly concentrated on my own performance, looking out from the stage and responding to the effect of my actions, rather than considering those of the ensemble.

Initially we performed at a small theatre called The Royal Victoria Hall in Southborough, which was very traditional with a beautifully decorated proscenium arch, large stage and two small dressing rooms behind. The auditorium had a balcony and there was a small foyer and box office at the front – it was a perfect little hall, now sadly demolished. Within those walls we performed Noel Coward's' Present Laughter', 'Oh! What a Lovely War!', 'Equus', 'Death of a Salesman' and others, so we didn't go for the safe 'Am-Dram' choices. Later we started using a new theatre in the centre of Tunbridge Wells that had been converted from a de-consecrated church, the Trinity Arts Centre, and that gave us more flexibility to stage productions in ever more experimental ways. It had a lovely auditorium with steeply raked seating rising from a floor-level stage, and when it was full created an incredible atmosphere. At Trinity we continued to stage some great drama, with productions of 'Educating Rita' and 'A Day in the Death of Joe Egg', as well as moving towards our own originally scripted shows. One Christmas DTW even staged a production of *A Christmas Carol,* and I took on the role of the narrator, aka Charles Dickens, and for the very first time opened a show with the words 'Marley was dead, to begin with.' Little did I know then how that sentence would become such a large part of my life.

Theatre was where I was at my happiest and I continued to get involved in as many productions as I could. I learned my craft by listening and observing and soaking up the experience of those who had been involved for many years. I learned how to project, instead of shouting, I learned how to stand, how to turn, how to engage with other characters on the stage and how to become part of a team.

In 1981 I left Huntley's School and continued my education at a nearby college, where I studied English, history and most importantly drama. I spent my days with a group of like-minded students, all taking the whole thing terribly seriously, all believing that we were going to change the world. Our year, as probably is every year at every drama school, was divided between those who favoured the Brechtian style of theatre and those who followed Stanislavski's 'method'. We learned how to delve into a text to discover what might lie beneath the words on the page – every character has their own back story, and it was always fun to either discover or invent it as a means of creating a more completely rounded performance. Even today with *A Christmas Carol* I still explore the possible backgrounds of some of the minor characters, to see if I can find a new angle.

Each year the college performed a musical which meant that all aspects of the Creative Arts department would have an opportunity to show off their talents, and one of the productions during my time there was 'Robert and Elizabeth' which told the story of the love affair between Robert Browning and Elizabeth Barret. It was quite a sombre affair, tending towards the operatic, and I was cast as Robert Surtees-Cook, a chinless wonder of an army officer who provided a little comic light relief. I only had one song in the show, which was more spoken than sung, in the Rex Harrison style (I am not a natural musician or singer). The orchestral introduction to 'Hate Me Please' is what is known as a 'till ready', in other words the musicians just repeat a particular musical phrase under the dialogue and when the singer is ready to launch into the song they start at the beginning of the next repeat. Unfortunately, I was not confident in my musical abilities and at the first dress rehearsal kept missing the start of the phrase and had to wait for it to come round again. I became more and more nervous as I missed the beat each time, so sending the orchestra around over and over again. I could see from the face of our conductor, Mrs Budden, that she was neither sympathetic nor impressed with my efforts as she glared up at me thrusting her baton at me as the start point arrived once more. At last, I metaphorically shut my eyes and jumped, I don't think it was at the right moment and there was a scrabbling of the musicians to get to the same point in the song that I was at. 'Hate me please! I'd be a happy chappy if you'd hate me please,' was the opening line and I am sure that the entire music department embraced the sentiment wholeheartedly.

I learned another lesson during Robert and Elizabeth and that involved the use, and possible pitfalls, of radio microphones. At the end of the first act the actor playing the sickly Elizabeth Barret was subsiding onto her bed apparently on the point of death, indeed she only just had enough breath left in her to belt out a soaring aria to bring the half to a close. The curtain fell as she dramatically slumped down. Backstage we all piled into the dressing room and drank water, chatted about the first half, read books and did all of the things that actors do in dressing rooms. The second act would begin exactly where we had left the story, so the curtain arose to reveal the unconscious Elizabeth slumped on her chaise longue. Unfortunately, the backstage communication wasn't as good as it should have been and while the stage manager was sending word to the tech box and the orchestra that the act was ready to begin, the actor playing Elizabeth was still chatting in the dressing room. In a moment she heard the orchestra begin the Entr'acte and realising that she should be on the stage let out a very loud and dirty expletive, as she ran to the wings. Unfortunately, up in the tech box the sound engineer had turned her microphone on, fully expecting the curtain to rise and her to begin signing again, meaning that the audience were treated to a most un-Elizabeth Barret-like soliloquy! To this day I err on the side of caution when dealing with wireless mics, even if it has sometimes led to me not turning them on before a show.

Also at college I became part of a sort of fringe review company, the Wot No Players, and performed in a comic double act with the group's founder Alastair Hutchinson. Alastair and I had sketches based around two country singers, Slim Willy and Prentis Dirk. As far as I can remember we only had two songs, one based on the children's song 'Three Little Fishes', and the other on 'In an English Country Garden'. I seem to remember that we thought our scripts hilarious, but I am very sure that the audiences, other than our drama-student entourage, did not.

After I had left college, my theatrical career was sparse – I tried to involve myself in any productions that I could find, as an actor and later as a director, but I couldn't claim that it was my profession. To pay the bills I worked as a driving instructor, but my passion was always on the stage, and I kept my hand in by performing and directing with various local amateur theatre groups.

Eventually I began to work part time as a performer at a

local tourist attraction, where I would greet the visitors in the character of a Georgian street sweeper and over the years I learned the skills of improvisation for not only were visitors interested in the historical facts that I had carefully learned, but also wanted to know where the nearest grocery store, ATM or public toilet facilities were located - it was not always easy to answer in the Georgian vernacular! It was during those years that, along with other performers from the attraction, we formed a corporate theatrical company that specialised in murder mystery evenings, and the like. Once again it was great training, especially for thinking on your feet, for you never knew what questions you may be asked, and it was essential to maintain the character as you searched for the words necessary to move the plot on.

Apart from the murder mystery events we also signed a contact with the Kent Police training college, to provide roleplay actors for various training scenarios. The scripts would be written by the training team and were designed to help the candidates learn the correct procedure for dealing with various commonplace situations which they may eventually be called upon to deal with. On one occasion a young officer was given a situation of having witnessed some erratic driving, presumably under the influence of alcohol. The imaginary car had car pulled up in an imaginary car park at an imaginary leisure centre, and, in the scripted scenario, the driver walked unsteadily inside. What the young officer was supposed to do was to approach the suspect and ask him if he had been drinking, then he was supposed to use his radio to call for a drink-driving testing kit. At this point, having been satisfied that the young candidate demonstrated the correct radio technique, the trainer would hand over a kit, and then the exercise would proceed, testing the knowledge of breathalyser procedure. Our candidate came nervously into the room, and uncertainly navigated the opening exchanges (I was playing the supposed drunk driver, so gently slurred a few words to help him along). Eventually he reached the moment when he would need to test me but became aware that there was no testing kit to hand. He floundered around for a while, until the ever-patient trainer whispered – 'Use your radio!' The young officer looked confused for a moment, then unclipped the radio from his shoulder and approached me, intent on sticking the aerial into my mouth, and asking me to blow! When he finally finished the exercise and left the room, the trainer removed his glasses, wiped his brow, and said, 'there goes a future Chief Constable!' There were many similar anecdotes during those years and we had great fun with the police force.

As fun as those years were, I realise now that they were training for what was to come next.

Chapter 2
The Skipping Stone: Discovering Charles

My life changed completely in May 1993, with an inconsequential meeting with a lady called Elizabeth who was responsible for raising money to preserve an historic village hall in the county of Kent.

1993 marked the 150th anniversary of the first publication of *A Christmas Carol*, and even though the celebrations would begin in November, Elizabeth was a forward-thinking lady and approached me with a proposition: Charles Dickens had loved acting and indeed had performed *A Christmas Carol* during his reading tours. I was an actor. There would be a lot of publicity surrounding the book that Christmas, and she needed a high-profile fundraising event – would I recreate one of Charles Dickens' readings for her?

To be honest, I wasn't keen, for I hadn't enjoyed a close relationship with my great-great-grandfather up to that point. Our house had always been filled with Dickensian books and memorabilia, my father was a great fan and a great scholar, but he never forced his passion onto his children. His mantra was that we should do the best at whatever we wanted to do, whether that was journalism, as was the case with my eldest sister Liz, photography for my brother Ian, catering and hotel management with Nicky and theatre with me. 'Mind you,' he would occasionally add with a twinkle in his eyes, 'you will discover Dickens one day…' And he was right, of course, we all did in our own ways.

I had first become aware of the importance of our ancestor on 9 June, 1970, exactly one hundred years after Charles had died of a massive stroke in his home at Gad's Hill Place in Kent. The great and the good of Britain were keen to celebrate and honour one of their national institutions, and the Dickens family was invited to Westminster Abbey to attend a service of thanksgiving for his life. Ian was dressed in smart suit, as was my father. Nicky was in a dress typical of the early seventies, and my mother wore a hat. We were accompanied by my aging Grandmother, Pearl, who would die just a few months later. Me? I wore a shirt and tie, and a pair of shorts, with polished sandals. My hair was brushed carefully, and I had no real idea as to the import of what was going on. Poor Liz, the eldest of the four, was not with us, as her school refused permission for her to miss an examination scheduled for that day – ironically it was for English Literature.

Once we were in the Abbey we sat in the front pew, but nothing seemed to happen for a while, until suddenly we all stood again, and I became aware that Queen Elizabeth, the Queen Mother was taking her place in the very same pew as us and my six-year-old eyes opened widely: I knew her! I had seen her on the television! This Dickens man must be important if she was here! I am sure that we must have been introduced to her after the service, but I have no memory of that, just that flash of realisation when she took her place next to our family.

So, throughout my childhood I had a perception of who Charles Dickens was, and whenever the BBC made a new adaptation of one of the novels we would dutifully sit down and watch, although my attention would have wandered quickly, and I am sure that I disappeared to play in my bedroom with my Scalextric racing set, rather than learning the finer points of David Copperfield, or whatever it may have been.

I was much older the next time Dickens came into my life, for I was at secondary school, maybe aged fourteen or fifteen. It was September, and a new academic year was beginning, and we all filed into a classroom for the first English Literature class of the year. Our teacher took up her position at the front of the class and commanded our attention, before commencing the lesson: 'This year we are going to study *'Oliver Twist'* by Charles Dickens. You will like it. 'It is a classic!' We groaned, for a classic meant that we wouldn't understand it, and that the teacher would point out the 'humour' within the impenetrable text, which would be anything but funny.

The fact that the book mentioned was *'Oliver Twist'* meant nothing to me, it could have been *'Henry V'*, *'Cider with Rosie'* (although that was a bit naughty we would later discover), or any other of the books that were selected for us, until the teacher continued: 'It was written by Dickens's great-great-grandfather, Charles Dickens!' Every eye in the room bored down on me in sheer fury, and my sole emotion about Dickens' ground-breaking second novel was guilt for inflicting this on my classmates.

I never finished reading the novel and, if I remember correctly, actually quoted lyrics from Lionel Bart's musical adaptation of the book in my final exam, little knowing that the character of Fagin, far from being the cheerful figure of fun with all of the best songs, was one of the darkest, most manipulative villains imaginable, and almost all of the woes of early Victorian society were collected on his shoulders.

Maybe my name impressed the examiners, or perhaps I understood more that I realised, for at the end of the year I passed the exam with a decent enough mark.

Looking back, it seems as if my connections with Dickens were like a stone skimming across the surface of a still lake, and as time went on those little skips came closer together before finally uniting completely.

The final skip came in 1980 with a visit to the theatre. In the June of that year The Royal Shakespeare Company had opened a new production of Nicholas Nickleby, and it was the talk of the theatrical community. The traditional way to adapt classic novels has always been to take a single strand of the plot, probably make it into a musical, and stick an exclamation mark on the end of a single word title (Nickleby had already received this treatment with the 1973 musical 'Smike!' And of course, 'Oliver!' was almost more famous than *'Oliver Twist, or The Parish Boy's Progress'* when it took the West End by storm in 1960 and then was made as a film in 1968). The RSC however, didn't want to take such liberties with the original text and were determined to tell the story as Dickens had written it. An ensemble was engaged, and basic casting took place, although most actors would be required to play multiple roles. Small groups were sent off with specific scenes from the book and were asked to improvise until they had something that could be performed to the rest of the company. The actors, unconstrained by a script, created scenes in which the rich narrative of the author accompanied the dialogue, and it soon became apparent that if this production should ever make it to the stage, it would not be a short show. In fact, when Nickleby opened its running time was 8 ½ hours, and it was presented as two self-contained performances, which could be seen on different days.

When the show first opened the critical reaction was not good, (even though the audiences flocked to see it), and maybe this was the reason that the Dickens family were invited en

45

masse to see the show on New Year's Eve 1980 (that and the fact that anyone with any sense was out partying, leaving the Aldwych theatre potentially empty). I was eighteen and couldn't think of anything worse than being made to sit through almost nine hours of Dickens (of course, we were seeing the whole thing in a single day, during a matinee and evening session), instead of doing what most teenagers do on New Year's Eve.

We took our seats and instantly I was amazed as members of the cast mingled with the audience, chatting, laughing, and apparently trying to sell us very stale muffins, until almost without warning they gathered on stage at a public meeting to incorporate the United Metropolitan Improved Hot Muffin and Crumpet Baking and Delivery Company. There was life and action and fun and loud brash characters. Within five minutes of the show starting I was completely hooked and sat on the edge of my seat as the various stories of Nicholas, Smike, Kate, Ralph and all of the others unfolded before my eyes. Suddenly Dickens meant something to me, for his work was pure theatre and I loved every second.

The first part came to an end with a hilarious production of Romeo and Julliet performed by the members of Mr Vincent Crummles' theatre troupe, and I could barely wait for the second section to begin.

The skipping pebble sank to the bed of the lake, and I had become a born-again Dickens: Hallelujah!

Back to 1993, and I had agreed to perform the reading to celebrate 150 years of *A Christmas Carol*. I soon realised what a rash decision that was, in that I knew very little about Dickens, and I had never performed any form of one-man theatre, not even a monologue. I felt woefully underprepared

46

for such a performance. What I did have, however, was an expert to hand, so sat down with my father to ask his advice, which came in two parts. Firstly, he gave me a 'reading copy' of *A Christmas Carol*, that was based on the version that Charles himself had edited for performance. If one were to read the entire book it would take about four hours, which even for *'The Inimitable'* (as Dickens modestly called himself) was far too long, so a shortened version would be essential and what better place to start than to use the edition containing as much as the author himself had decided was necessary to effectively tell the story? It was also the version that I had listened to as a five-year-old when my Uncle Claud read to us on Christmas Eve.

The second bit of advice from Dad didn't appear to be as helpful as I had hoped. I asked 'how should I perform it? How do I create different characters? How will the audience know what is happening?' To which my father simply said, 'Remember that Charles Dickens has done all of the work for you.' Which was not quite what I'd been hoping for.

I took the book and started reading it, aloud, to see what would happen. The language in the opening chapters certainly created an eery and dark atmosphere which would definitely convince the audience that they were being guided through a ghost story, but there was still the issue of making the multiple characters live. I flipped the pages until I arrived at the first description of Ebenezer Scrooge:

'Oh! But he was a tight-fisted hand at the grindstone, Scrooge! a squeezing, wrenching, grasping, scraping, clutching, covetous, old sinner! Hard and sharp as flint, from which no steel had ever struck out generous fire; secret, and self-contained, and solitary as an oyster. The cold within him froze his old features, nipped his pointed nose, shrivelled his cheek, stiffened his gait; made his eyes red, his thin lips blue; and spoke out shrewdly in his grating voice.

'External heat and cold had little influence on him. No warmth could warm, no wintry weather chill him. No wind that blew was bitterer than he, no falling snow was more intent upon its purpose, no pelting rain less open to entreaty. The heaviest rain, and snow, and hail, and sleet, could boast of the advantage over him in only one respect. They often "came down" handsomely, and Scrooge never did.' (this from the edited 'reading' version, rather than from the original)

Just a single reading of that description and I had transformed into Scrooge – my face had contorted, my body stiffened and more importantly my voice had cracked into that of old Ebenezer. My father had been correct in that Dickens had done the work for me. I will explain about other characterisations later in the book, but back in '93 I was able to build up my performance using the stage directions that Charles Dickens had given to me in the text.

Although I had been commissioned to recreate Dickens' performances of *A Christmas Carol*, I actually decided it would be much more effective if I performed it in a way that seemed natural to me, and therefore didn't undertake any further research into what he had done – this was to be my interpretation of his own script, rather than any attempt at an impersonation, which seemed somewhat pointless as nobody would know if it was accurate or not.

Apart from the vocal performance, with distinct voices for each of the characters, I also felt I needed to add a sense of physicality to the show, to lift it from the page. Being stood at a reading desk meant that my left hand was not available, as it would be holding the book, so any gestures I used would have to be made with my right hand alone. Initially I simply developed a series of points, which differed for each ghost: with Jacob Marley I tried to capture the transparency of his appearance, whilst maintaining the sense of strength and command of his character, whilst the Ghost of Christmas Past's movements were ethereal and gossamer-like. Present was big, brash and bold, whereas the Ghost of Christmas Yet to Come just pointed onward with a single, skeletal finger, remembering the DTW exercise of years before. Even today when I reach this point in the script, my arm is locked solid, and even occasionally prone to cramp.

During the year I didn't return to the project much, but a tentative phone call from Elizabeth, towards the end of October asking how the show was progressing reminded me that I had plenty of work to do, and my schooldays memory of standing on stage alone, vulnerable as the audience laughed at me gave me motivation aplenty to do the best job possible. I returned to the reading copy and rehearsed each scene, making notes in the margins along the way to assist me. Some passages I deleted, and other phrases that Dickens had omitted, I re-inserted.

The show was to be held at the Chiddingstone Village Hall, in the county of Kent on the 10 and 11 of December. To create atmosphere the room was lit by candles, while the aroma of fresh fir and holly mingled with that of mulled wine and mice pies. I don't remember anything of the build-up, I don't remember if I was nervous, although I imagine I must have been. I do remember worrying about the very low lighting and whether I would actually be able to see my reading book, for the rehearsals in the hall had been carried out in the daylight, and now a winter's darkness had enveloped the village.

I also remember feeling that as soon as I started reading I felt at home, and of course my father had been correct, Dickens was with me and helping me. Each scene ran seamlessly into the next and the story moved along with a great pace. At one point I noticed that at one of the tables (the room was laid out in a cabaret style), a gentleman scribbled a note on a napkin and passed it to a companion, who having read it, wrote a reply and handed it back. I felt a surge of excitement and pride to think that the audience were desperate to discuss the show but didn't want to break the atmosphere by using words! It was obvious to me that I had succeeded in captivating the room. When the show came to an end, and the audience had left, I made my way to the table to discover what glowing review had been written about the performance, and on reading the note I came crashing down to earth once more, for it read: 'Is he going to read the whole bloody book?' to which the reply was 'God, I hope not!'

However, the performance had been a success, with lots of positive feedback and it certainly seemed to be something worth pursuing in future years.

Throughout the next year I decided to investigate the possibilities of performing some other pieces by Charles Dickens, and once again my father came to my aid by buying me a copy of 'Sikes and Nancy and Other Readings.' This slim paperback contained all the readings that Dickens had performed during his touring years, and my attention was immediately drawn to 'Nicholas at the Yorkshire School'. Since my interest in the works of my great-great-grandfather had been awoken by the stage adaptation of Nickleby, this script, which featured the brilliant characters of Wackford Squeers, his daughter Fanny, her best friend Tilda Price, the bluff Yorkshireman John Browdie, not to mention Nicholas and Smike, seemed like an excellent starting point. Dad introduced me to the Rochester and Chatham branch of the Dickens Fellowship and it was with an air of great uncertainty that I attended one of their regular meetings to perform for them. The meeting was held in the Guildhall in Rochester High Street and the members of the branch were a knowledgeable lot, to be sure – there would be nowhere to hide.

As with *A Christmas Carol* I decided not to research Dickens' own performances of the piece, but to read it in a way that suited my particular style, although many of the voices and mannerisms were 'borrowed' from the RSC. Again, the reading was successful, drawing many positive comments, and I was invited by the Medway Council to perform at the forthcoming Rochester Dickens Festival. In the hastily prepared publicity material that I had thrown together I had used a few quotes about Charles' performances, including one from the great Victorian tragedian William Charles Macready, who gushed that Dickens had been 'the greatest reader of the greatest writer of the age.' Come the festival I was horrified to see that this quote had been used to describe me! Before commencing the reading, I explained the error to the audience, and then none to modestly added that for the moment I should perhaps be regarded as the 'second greatest reader of the greatest writer in the world' which, in hindsight, was in itself a rather high and mighty claim, considering that there are fine actors performing Dickens all over the world and, up to that point, I had read just three times.

I reprised my *A Christmas Carol* performance the next Christmas, and as a second full year as a Dickens performer came around, I felt that I needed to introduce something new to my repertoire and decided to write my own show about Dickens and his performances. I didn't want to create anything too serious or academic, so set out to produce a script that had variety, and some laughs. I built the show around various very theatrical characters, but I also included some letters written by both Dickens and his closest friends, and then bound the whole thing together with my own observations and narrative. When I had finally finished the piece, I printed it off and then realised with horror that I had just committed myself to learning a monologue of some twenty pages, whereas in the past the longest thing I'd ever had to learn was maybe a single page. I didn't know if I could do it, or not, but I set to learning each little section, before eventually linking them all together. I discovered that when I was reciting the lines I had to move and would pace back and forth whispering to myself, gradually building it up in my memory. It is a technique that worked for me then and one that I still use today.

I struggled slightly with the opening of the show. Originally it started with a bang - I would enter from the back of an auditorium in the character of Mr Crummles, the larger-than-life actor from Nickleby, as he conducts a rehearsal between two boys performing a sword fight. It is a great scene, but it didn't quite work, for the audience had no idea what was going on or how they were supposed to react. I needed to let them know that it was OK to laugh and to be a little irreverent. I had to find a way of reassuring an audience that they were in safe hands. Eventually the solution came to me thanks to a member of The Dickens Fellowship organisation, who knew everything there was to know about Charles Dickens. I knew that Thelma Grove would be present at one of my performances and I decided that I wanted to include a quote from Dickens that she had never read. Of course, this was an impossibility, for Thelma was not only well versed in Dickens' work, but his life too, so there only one thing for it, I would have to make a quote up.

The new opening of Mr Dickens is Coming! saw me welcome the audience, tell them that the performance was centred on Dickens' theatrical career and before I began I would like to read to them the words of Charles Dickens. I would seriously open a small book, flick a few pages as if searching for the passage in question, take a deep breath and begin:

'Throughout my lifetime, as boy, youth and man, I have derived a love of the stage. Today I am fortunate to stand upon the great stages of the world, and to read from my own works. I pray that when my lifetime is done my characters may still live on these same stages. This, then, is my legacy to my family; those members known to me today and those descendants whom I shall never meet. May they take the pleasures that I have taken from the institution of the theatre!'

I would then slowly close the book and pause as if to let the true significance of those words sink in. Then I would look at the audience and say 'As I said, those were the words of Charles John Huffam Dickens.' I would look at the closed book, before adding, 'unfortunately for me, he never actually used them in that particular order, but they were all his words at some stage or another throughout his lifetime!'

It was the perfect opening, and immediately allowed the audience to laugh out loud, and reassured them that what followed was not going to be too serious. When I first performed it for Thelma, I watched her closely, and as the bogus quote continued, I could see her looking more and more confused, until I delivered the punch line, at which moment her expression cleared and she laughed loudly with the rest of them, giving me a little nod of approval as she did so.

Over the years since I have introduced many new performances, and in the early days most were inspired by the knowledge that my father imparted. He would love to watch me perform but got very nervous and would need to stand at the back of a room, rather than sitting in the bulk of the audience. The nervousness on his part led to a sort of hyperactivity and his hand would be constantly moving, so he thrust them deep into his jacket pockets which inevitably were full of loose change. From the stage I could easily tell how worried my father was by the volume of the jangling - the more nervous he was, the more loudly he rattled those coins!

My new career in England was developing nicely, but things were about to change for ever, as a new chapter in my life opened.

Chapter 3
Coming to America

I had not initially considered performing my readings of *A Christmas Carol* anywhere except in Britain, but it was once again my father who steered me in a direction that would dominate my life for the next thirty years.

The story started in 1974 in Galveston, Texas where members of the Galveston Historical Foundation, an organisation dedicated to the preservation and regeneration of the historic downtown area of the island city, decided to stage a Christmas festival to raise funds and awareness. Feeling that the festival should have a theme the Foundation decided to utilize the name of the main thoroughfare - The Strand, which took its name from the street in London. So, a Christmas festival with an attachment to London led to the marketing team tapping into America's love affair with Charles Dickens and *A Christmas Carol,* therefore the festival was christened 'Dickens on the Strand', even though Charles never wrote about, or visited Texas. The temperatures in Galveston in December are warm and pleasant so it was decided to make 'Dickens' an open-air event, with the city sealing off a large area to traffic. Vendors would be able to rent space and booths to hawk their wares, whilst several stages were to be erected so that there could be a constant programme of music and entertainment throughout the weekend. Actors in exquisite Victorian costumes were booked to walk the streets and a

Grand Parade would be held with Queen Victoria and Prince Albert at its head.

Visitors to the festival would have to pay an entrance fee to attend, but the board took an inspired decision to give a fifty per cent discount for anyone wearing Victorian costume. Everyone likes a bargain, so it was assured that the streets would be filled with young urchins in caps and tatty waistcoats and pretty maidens in recycled bridesmaid's dresses. Back in 1974 My father's cousin and Charles' great granddaughter Monica Dickens was living on Cape Cod and accepted an invitation to attend the inaugural festival thereby beginning the tradition of there being a member of the Dickens family at every event. After Monica the ebullient Cedric Dickens took over for a few years after which he passed the baton on to my father, who attended with my mother at his side. During his tenure Dad presided over a great banquet during which he would regale the guests with readings from *A Christmas Carol*. My parents also took pride of place in the Grand Parade, sitting in a horse drawn coach waving to the cheering crowds. Mum and dad loved their time at Galveston and embraced the America zeal to do things on a giant scale with relish.

However, despite the enjoyment they found at the festival itself, my parents did not enjoy the travelling, and unbeknown to me had taken the decision not to return to Galveston in '94. During that summer one of the senior board members from the Historical Foundation was visiting England, and Dad invited her to lunch. When the date was fixed, he asked me if I could arrange a performance of my show somewhere for her to watch. I found a venue, a private room above a pub in Tunbridge Wells, and a goodly crowd of friends and curious members of the public attended to see *A Christmas Carol* performed in the middle of August.

I wore a simple suit and tie for that show, no costume, and there were no props or decorations to make the room in anyway Christmassy, but the performance went very well, and the audience laughed and applauded loudly. If this had been an audition, then it was a successful one, for I was invited to Galveston to take on the mantle of Dickens representative at the 1994 event.

It seems extraordinary now, but the arrangements for that first visit were made in just a couple of months. My old friend Paul Standen, who had been one of the leaders of the DTW theatre group, came on board as a manager. Paul worked in the City of London in one of the large international banks, and was blessed with a clear, logical mind, as well as a great understanding as to what actors and performers needed, being one himself, so was an excellent ally to discuss terms and arrangements with the various organisations that I would be working with. Paul and I also worked with the Charles Dickens Museum in London to buy a stock of the reading edition of *A Christmas Carol*, the same edition that formed the core of my show. It had originally been published, with a white cover, in 1965, and had been re-issued with a red cover in 1970, it was now undergoing a third iteration in green, to celebrate the 150th anniversary.

The main contact was of course the Galveston Historical Foundation, but there were two other venues who were interested in my performances too, one was The Kansas City Holiday Fair, on which Dad had worked as a consultant, and a private home in Atlanta also.

American Airlines was a sponsor of The Galveston event, and thus I was flown business class from Britain to Atlanta, a treat that was not to be repeated too often in subsequent years!

An early publicity shot

Photo Credit: Author's Collection

Atlanta

My first stop was in the rarefied neighbourhood of Buckhead in Atlanta, where the Governor of the state of Georgia has his mansion, and where the most affluent folk live. I had been booked by a lady called Beth Ventulett to read during an Open Christmas House event that she was organising.

As the plane began descending into Atlanta's airport I vividly remember being overcome by a wave of nervousness. I looked down at the houses beneath me and whispered under my breath 'can I give those people what they want?' It was a form of stage fright, although fortunately not on the stage.

I was met at the airport by Beth and her husband Tom, who were charming hosts and who took me under their wing. The day after my arrival Tom took me on a driving tour of downtown Atlanta and along the way he would occasionally point out some huge skyscraper and say, 'that's one of mine'. Tom was one of the city's leading architects and he was responsible for creating much of Atlanta's modern skyline.

On the day of the event, we went to a large and impressive house where the young owners had been moved out so that the professional designers and decorators could move in. It was raining hard, and everyone was rushing around trying to prepare the home. One lady pushed past me in her haste, then stopped and looked back: 'Oh! you are the Dickens guy? I thought that you would be older and fatter' and then off she went to do whatever it was she had to do. Quite the introduction, and I have never been entirely sure if she was impressed or disappointed by my age and build.

The performance itself was given from the home's feature staircase, with the audience gathered in the hallway beneath me. Afterwards I spent plenty of time sat at a table signing copies of *A Christmas Carol* for the various guests, each of whom had very specific requests as to how the volume should be dedicated.

In researching this book, I found my original copy of the reading edition of *A Christmas Carol* complete with my pencil margin notes and editing, and on the title page Beth had signed it for me: 'To one of the most genteel fellows Atlanta has had the privacy of entertaining. Beth Ventulett'

Having given my one performance in Atlanta it was time to fly onto Houston, and from there I began my relationship with The Galveston Historical Foundation.

Galveston

My four years in Galveston have become all mixed together in my memory but it followed a well-trodden path which had been prepared and honed over the previous twenty-five years. During the week prior to the event (always held on the first weekend in December), there was lots of promotional work to be done, for Dickens on the Strand had a huge catchment area, and I was driven to TV stations in Houston to the north and to the southwest over the state line to Louisiana. One day was given to visiting a large children's hospital, so that all the costumed characters could bring the festival to desperately ill kids. I remember being so moved as we chatted as cheerfully as we could to tiny figures surrounded by monitors and drips. There was a young magician and juggler with us who was brilliant with the children, and I think that he was my first glimpse of the sheer enthusiasm and ebullience of American entertainers.

My main performance was on the Friday night before the weekend of the festival itself, and was held in Ashton Villa, an 1859 mansion belonging to the Foundation, and which boasted a ballroom that had been added in the 1920s. During my parents' years of attending, the Friday night banquet had become a highlight of the weekend and was a high-priced ticket event based around a little book that they had published called *Christmas with Dickens*, which laid down the framework for a traditional Christmas party, with short readings from *A Christmas Carol* to be performed between each dinner course. The book did not only feature the passages to be read, but also menu ideas, traditional recipes and descriptions of games which as a family we had played around our own Christmas table. It was a simple, self-published volume, wire-bound, and featured brilliant pen and ink illustrations by my brother Ian.

Dad had elevated this simple little idea into an entire production, working closely with the chef and his team who catered the event so that the timing would be perfect. As the evening went on there would be parades of the giant turkey and a flaming Christmas pudding, bringing cheers and laughter to the old property.

My job, therefore, was to try and replicate this huge success but in a way that left my own stamp on it. At every event in Galveston everyone greeted me warmly and then said 'Oh, we sure do miss your father, he was such a fun guy!' which although lovey to hear, put a great deal of pressure on my shoulders. When I later mentioned this to dad he laughed and said it had been exactly the same when he first attended: 'Great to meet you David, oh but we sure do miss Cedric, such a great guy!'

I did my own thing, and gave my performance in my own flamboyant style, utilising all the voices and gestures that I had perfected during the previous year. As far as I could tell the evening was a great success and I had taken a small step to forging my own identity in Galveston.

The festival itself was a blast – the streets filled with folk enjoying the warm weather, and I strolled around watching the various shows and embracing the atmosphere of a huge open-air party. My responsibilities during the weekend were limited to presenting myself at the Historical Foundation's offices to undertake book signings, and then to ride in a carriage with Queen Victoria at the head of the grand parade and to wave at the huge crowds.

For my first visit to Galveston I was accommodated in a hotel, but in the second and subsequent years I was given a room in one of the historic homes, where some of the costumed performers stayed. I shared the 1838 Menard Mansion with three others, Queen Victoria (played by a Houston based actress called Anne Boyd) as well as George and Kenny who represented a wax work museum in Victoria, British Columbia, and who had made the drive across the continent complete with a life-size representation of Charles Dickens for company. The move from a hotel to the house made me feel so good about what I was doing there, for it cast me as an actor, rather than as a VIP guest.

It was in that house that I experienced the closest thing to a haunting that I can remember. It was a Saturday night and the four of us had spent a busy day smiling and waving and engaging with the huge crowds. By the time we returned to the house we were exhausted and having changed out of our costumes, we slumped into chairs in the parlour. We chatted about our 'normal' lives, and I mentioned the series of Dickens shows that I was now developing in Britain. Anne was particularly interested to hear about Sikes and Nancy, the reading that Charles Dickens had performed which used the brutal murder of poor Nancy from Oliver Twist as its theme. I had recently started performing 'The Murder' and happened to have a copy of the script with me, so offered to read it for them.

The setting was perfect: a Victorian parlour, with the curtains and shutters closed against the dark night. I began.

The script that Dickens developed is a fascinating one, in that the actual violence of the murder is taken up in a very short passage, but the tension and the danger of the atmosphere is built up gradually as if it were the screen play for a psychological thriller in the Hitchcock style. In my show the actual act of murder is a sudden violent flashpoint and I bring my fist crashing down onto the book, and on that night as I reached the climax all of the lights in the house went out. Yes, as my fist met the book there was a complete blackout throughout the old home. We stumbled through the rooms into the hallway and found the fuse box, which for some reason had tripped, and soon we were bathed in light again, but the shock of the moment had affected us all, and I didn't continue with the reading. We all retired to our rooms somewhat wide-eyed!

On the next morning when we arrived at the Historical Foundation's offices (which also acted as a green room for the performers), we mentioned our experience of the previous night, and the staff laughed and were not in the slightest bit surprised: 'Oh that would have been Clara! She hates anything violent to happen in her house.' The team went on to gleefully tell the story of Clara Menard, the daughter of the house's owner. On a certain evening she had been preparing for a grand ball, some said maybe it was even her wedding day, and walked to the top of the stairs in her gown, where she tripped and fell down the staircase, breaking her neck as she did so. By the time she lay at the foot of the stairs, she was dead. Since that day, the folk in the office told us, Clara's spirit had remained in the house and made her displeasure plain if anything untoward should be happening – The Murder of Nancy would have been a step too far for Clara Menard!

This was on Sunday, the final day of the festival and that evening Anne would be returning to Houston while Ken and George would be starting the drive back to Victoria, meaning that I would be spending Sunday night alone in the mansion.

When the festivities were over, I returned to the Menard House and changed. I spent the whole evening in the kitchen, the only modernised room in the house (the other rooms were beautifully preserved, for the house was open to visitors during the days), with all of the lights I could find blazing brightly. As the evening went on and I started to think about going upstairs to my bedroom, when I suddenly heard a noise from the hallway and went to investigate… a cascade of water was running down the stairs and was forming a pool in the hallway where Clara had supposedly lain dead…

It was with a sense of relief that I left the house the next morning and took a ride to the airport. Later the Galveston folk told me that an upstairs cistern had overflowed, causing the running water, and they had greatly enjoyed the CCTV footage of me mopping up the mess with towels, looking over my shoulders constantly with an expression of confused fear on my face!

Being a strictly historical organisation, the need to deal in fact is always uppermost in GHF's mission, and to counterbalance the fable, the staff told have since told me the truth behind Clara Menard's life, pointing out that she married a man from Alabama during the Civil War and died from Yellow Fever whilst staying with her new in-laws, her husband being away fighting for the South. Whatever the reality of Clara's life, I shall never forget the chill that sat upon me after the Menard Mansion had demonstrated its displeasure at my reading 'The Murder' from *Oliver Twist*.

The other lasting memory of my time in Galveston is a

happier one and features a slice of Key lime pie, eaten as I sat on a restaurant terrace looking out across the Gulf of Mexico. It was sublime and every other Key lime pie I have eaten since falls short of that first benchmark.

On to Kansas City

From my initial visit to Galveston in 1994 I then flew on to Kansas City, Missouri for the final leg of my first trip and this was to attend another event that my parents had been a central part of.

During his years at Galveston, Dad had met with some folk who either came from Kansas City or had relatives there, I don't recall which, but who were keen to stage a similar event in Missouri. Of course, the December weather in the Mid-West is not quite as reliable as that on the Gulf coast, so the new event would be held indoors, with a large downtown convention centre being picked as a suitable venue. To ensure a Victorian atmosphere the Missouri Rep theatre company were brought on board to build huge sets representing London street scenes, as well as providing costumes for Dickensian characters. Dad was invited to be a consultant on all things Dickens and had thrown himself into the project. The Dickens Holiday Fair launched in 1993 and Mum and Dad were there, at the centre of everything, signing, reading, parading, as they had been in Texas.

Although I arrived in Kansas City on Monday morning, the Holiday Fair was not due to open until the following Friday meaning that I had four unfilled days ahead of me. There was a certain amount of media work to do but the organisers of the fair rather wanted me out in the community spreading the word, rather than lounging in a hotel suite doing nothing, so they contacted the board of the Mid-Continent Public Library

Service and suggested that I make appearances in a couple of branches. I could do a reading as well as talking about the weekend's event and try to encourage guests to visit.

The Mid-Continent Public Library Service is based in Independence, Missouri and has branches dotted all around the perimeter of downtown Kansas City and I was to be driven from one branch to another, giving performances and generally talking about the main event at the weekend.

My first evening's commitment was at Raytown Library and I remember it vividly for there was an awful ice storm that night. I had never seen anything like that before and across the city fires were breaking out as power cables came down under the weight of the ice. I seem to remember that we did a bit of Q&A on that occasion, and someone asked me, with a sense of incredulity, 'why did you come to Raytown?' I answered: 'The weather!' The marketing team at Mid Continent had done a good job and there was a reporter and photographer at the library and the next morning at breakfast my photo dominated the front page of the Kansas City Star's arts section. I was making a large expansive gesture, and the editor had cleverly cropped the picture so that you could not see the book in my other hand.

Like Galveston, the Kansas City Holiday Fair was a flamboyant affair, with many costumed characters walking the floors and interacting with the guests. There were two grand parades each day, as well as a 'Fezziwig's Ball' during which we were all expected

A true Dickens reads to students

Photo Credit: Author's Collection

to dance quadrilles and other country dances. I performed in a small theatre, that had been built into the spectacular set, and signed lots of copies of the 150th anniversary *A Christmas Carol*. Occasionally people would bring a book that my father had signed in previous years, and it always filled me with great emotion to see his spidery David Charles Dickens signature on a title page. Even to this day a copy will occasionally be brought to an event with dad's autograph in it and the effect is still the same on me.

When my parents had decided that they didn't want to travel any more, Dad wrote an account of their final trip and added a short appendix explaining some things that anyone who followed in his footsteps should be aware of. His advice on signing is fascinating to read now and is comprehensive in the extreme. He wrote fourteen paragraphs laying down his signing laws. Phrases such as:

'The person signing should have no responsibility whatever for crowd control. If he gets involved with this he may become unpleasantly with trouble-makers who bend the rules, or when the session has to be brought to an end.'

'The signer should have a personal assistant (in my case Betty). She welcomes the individuals coming to the desk, asks what they like written in the book, asks them how to spell it, writes it down on a slip of paper IN CAPITALS, and passes it to the signer. (People, especially if they are shy, speak softly, and you cannot always hear what they say. There are certain pitfalls in America, such as the letter "Z". We call it "zed"; they call it "zee". Oddly enough, American orthography is different from ours, and difficult to read. They seem not to be able to print what we call "Block Capitals".

'What will the signer write in the book... Some members of the public will request the oddest inscriptions such as "to my beloved wife Julie with my undying love" Such things should be categorically disallowed. One has to point out that whoever Julie is, she is not my beloved wife, and it is not <u>my</u> undying love, so that it is not appropriate for me to say that.'

'Start the session at precisely the advertised time, and end it at precisely the advertised time. When it is ended, get up and go. Bugger off somewhere very fast and disappear. Otherwise people will come running after you, and this will be unfair.'

Three pages of detailed instruction! For Dad the signing sessions were his event, that is what he was there for, whereas for me they are an extension of my show. I know that he found them extremely hard work, and when a book bearing his signature is presented to me now, I can always see when he was exhausted by the energy of his autograph.

The Dickens Holiday Fair in downtown Kansas City survived for four or five years but eventually the finance could not be found to sustain it and it faded away, but the relationship with the Mid-Continent Public Library Service survived, and continues to this day, making it my longest-standing relationship with an event sponsor.

Jackson Enterprises

Little did I know but during the first Galveston performance at Ashton Villa in 1994 there was someone in the audience who would change my life forever. Caroline Jackson was originally from Alabama and had worked as a journalist in Washington DC: the mixture of soft, generous southern belle and hardnosed businesswoman made her a formidable character, and she fought my corner for thirteen years.

Caroline was a true American entrepreneur and had bought the American rights to 'Christmas With Dickens' from my parents and Cedric, and was preparing to publish it. On hearing that my performances were based on the book's contents she saw that there was a marketing opportunity and invited me to lunch in Galveston. It was a blur to me, but she proposed the opportunity of becoming my American agent and booking an extensive tour of the country. The opportunities to me were boundless, she promised, but we would have to move very quickly if we were to get a tour together by 1995 – and so for the first and very definitely not for the last time, I found myself being out-manoeuvred by Caroline Jackson!

Within days of my arrival in the UK a contract arrived by fax (yes, it was that long ago) and it was detailed in the extreme and quite restrictive on my part. Clause upon clause had been wrapped up in impenetrable legalese by her attorney but what she offered was generous and promised a future that I could never have dreamed of a year before. I signed and have never regretted doing so.

Fortunately for me, my relationships with Galveston and Kansas City would remain in place, so there was some familiarity, but everything else was new to me. I wasn't an experienced traveller, by any means, and the world of check-ins, boarding, hotels, etc was alien to me.

My very first commitment with Caroline was not part of a Christmas tour, but at an event in Nashville, Tennessee, The Southern Festival of Books at which Caroline had arranged for me to perform Mr Dickens is Coming (the biographical show about Charles Dickens that I had written during the previous year) in the grand setting of the State Capitol building. Mr Dickens is Coming, you recall, is basically a show written to entertain – it is not academic or deeply artistic, but it is fun. As I waited to begin, I had the same doubts that I had experienced as I flew into Atlanta the year before: would this work, would the humour that had proved popular in Britain translate to an

American audience? Well, I needn't have worried for the show was a great success, and with a sense of relief I afterwards shared my concerns with an audience member who was gushing in his praise, and he seemed surprised by my fears, 'Oh, no, we LOVE British humour here…' my pride soared for an instant, until he added, 'Benny Hill is our favourite!' at which point my spirits dropped again – Benny Hill was a television entertainer of the 1970s, best known for smut and inuendo, his TV specials featuring casts of scantily-clad nubile young women being leered over by various lecherous older men… not exactly the profile I had hoped for with my new show!

1995 would be my first full Christmas (or 'Holiday', an expression previously unknown to me in the UK) tour with Caroline and apart from Galveston and Kansas City, she had put together an impressive schedule mainly featuring some very grand hotels. Once she had started marketing, Caroline had discovered that many venues, especially theatrical ones, were not keen on committing to an unknown and unproven product, so she was finding it difficult to fill the dates, but with a stroke of genius she struck up a deal with an organisation called The Historic Hotels of America Register, an umbrella group which promoted some of the most elegant, and of course, historic hotels in the United States. Press releases were sent out to every member hotel, describing my show, and in particular promoting the idea of showcasing the banqueting aspect of the property. My performances would fit between courses, as they had in Galveston, but the menu, the cost, the location and the timings were all decided by the hotel's own chef and banqueting staff. I would need to be flexible in my attitude and to adapt to whatever constraints were placed upon me on any given day. There was no flexibility, however, in

Caroline's ability to sell her books and gifts before and after the show – her contracts with the venues were very specific with details such as location of sales table, signage, and the exact form of words used in introductory remarks all rigidly prescribed, and woe betide anyone who didn't comply exactly.

The hotel gambit was successful and soon Caroline had arranged a full and exciting tour for me, but our naivety was about to be exposed.

I was a young, impressionable, wide-eyed actor being given the chance of a lifetime, and Caroline was an ambitious businesswoman, but with no background in international theatrical management: neither of us had any idea about the necessity of procuring a visa for my travels or completing any formal paperwork at all. I was due to fly into Dallas airport and from there connect to Vancouver for a brief visit to Victoria, before returning to the USA. After my long flight I joined the long line of passengers, clutching my passport in my hand and when I finally reached the desk the officer asked me what I was going to be doing whilst in the USA and I proudly announced that I was beginning a theatrical tour based on my own one man show of *A Christmas Carol*. He questioned me further about the length of my stay and the locations of my performances, and as he tapped his computer keyboard his expression became more concerned. Eventually he gave me my documents and told me to present myself at another office for 'secondary questioning', which didn't sound good. The office was filled with an assortment of characters, all of whom the USA government had deemed as some kind of threat. There were not only interviews being carried out, but complete searches too, very complete searches, although fortunately that was not deemed necessary for me.

The agent who took my case was kind, patient but firm,

and explained that to perform in America I needed a very specific type of visa that took around six months to be granted. Apparently, he informed me repeatedly, it was to prevent Mexican mariachi bands coming over the border and taking the work of American musicians (I assume that this was a particular issue in Dallas, and may have been less so in, for example, Boston). The upshot was that I would not be allowed to enter the USA without a visa. However, there was a very slight opportunity available to me, which was that from Dallas I was transferring immediately to Canada before arriving back to actually seek entrance to America in Los Angeles, but I would have to prove to immigration then that I had completed six months' worth of paperwork in three days. It didn't look good. With hindsight I think that the Dallas agent passed me on to his Californian colleagues because he didn't know how to deal with my case and didn't have the heart to actually refuse me entry. If I had been the guitarist of a mariachi band, however, I am sure he would have felt no such compulsion to be lenient.

Fortunately, I had managed to get a message to Caroline (this in the days before smart phones and instant communication), and she was already trying to work out how best to retrieve this situation as I boarded my flight from Dallas to Vancouver.

During my stay in Canada Caroline was her gracious self with our various hosts, but behind the scenes she was constantly on the phone, scribbling notes on the yellow legal notepads that she favoured. At one lunch at which I was the guest of honour, I was introduced to, I think, the British Ambassador in the city, and he promised to make representations on our behalf and indeed a few hours later I was called to a border post not far from Seattle and was asked to put my signature to a document which would allow me to return to the USA and perform. I was told in no uncertain terms that this was a once only 'free pass' and I would never be able to avail myself of the same opportunity again. For now, though, Caroline had secured the rest of the 1995 tour.

But there were further problems down the line. After the Christmas tour was completed, I was due to return to America in February, to celebrate Charles Dickens' birthday (he was born on 7 February 1812), at The Riverside Dickens Festival in California. There was no time to submit a Visa application, and certainly no time for one to be approved, so Caroline suggested to me that I attend Riverside as a guest performer, without receiving any payment, and in that way, I could not be regarded as a working actor. When the day to fly arrived I packed my suitcase with costumes and props for the various shows that I was due to perform (I remember that I was scheduled to do Nicholas Nickleby, so had a schoolmaster's cane in my case), and went to the airport to fly to Minneapolis/St Paul where I would clear immigration and then continue my journey on to Los Angeles.

When I arrived in The Twin Cities, I presented myself at the desk and once more I was asked to follow an officer to an office where I would be interviewed. This time the reception was not so friendly, and I was interrogated about my trip by a pair of officers: it wasn't the good cop, bad cop routine, for they were both stern, humourless, and unforgiving. 'What was I doing in America?' I was attending a festival. 'What would I be doing there?' Performing for the guests. 'What would they find in my luggage?' Costumes for my appearances. This fact was confirmed as they displayed the schoolmaster's cane in such a way as to suggest that it proved the depths of depravity I was bringing to the USA. 'Who was paying me?' I wasn't being paid; I was a guest. 'Where was I staying?' At the Mission Inn hotel in Riverside. 'Who was paying for the room?' The festival. 'Who had paid for my flight?' The festival. That was what the needed to know, for that meant I was receiving payment in kind – I was trying to enter the county illegally and was being renumerated for it. I was not to be permitted entry, I was to be sent home on the next available flight to England, and in the meantime, I would be kept under supervision. I was, in effect, a prisoner for a few hours.

When the flight boarded, I was escorted by the immigration officers, and my documents were handed directly to the captain in a sealed brown envelope. I was seated in the middle of the cabin, presumably so I couldn't make a dash for it at the last moment and was returned to my homeland once more.

In Riverside Caroline had already arrived, and when she knew what was going on, had to think on her feet once more. Apart from my public performances, I had been due to address the members of the Riverside business community on the subject of 'Dickens the Entrepreneur'. In an effort to make the best of a bad case, Caroline purchased a top hat from a local theatrical costumier and arranged for a phone link to be established between the hotel and my small home in Kent. In Riverside the top hat was sat on the podium from which I had been scheduled to speak, and my crackly words were broadcast into the ballroom, where the guests had no clue that I was actually sitting in my pyjamas, back home!

By the time I returned to America in November '96, Caroline had engaged an immigration attorney and we went through all of the correct channels to secure me a P3 Visa, which is 'a non-immigrant permit for artists or entertainers/performers who wish to come to the U.S. with the purpose of participating, sharing or developing any "culturally unique program".

The events of Dallas and Minneapolis would remain on my file, and for many years I was routinely taken aside for a secondary interview. Eventually, however, I was no longer deemed a threat to the USA and my record was cleared so that now my entrance to the country is a lot less complicated than once it was.

The Hotels

Caroline's arrangement with The Historic Hotels of America chain had yielded fruit and the list of hotels was impressive indeed, in those early years I performed at The Hotel Hershey, The Williamsburg Inn, The Peabody Hotel in Memphis, The Ojai Valley Inn and The Mission Inn in California and many others. Here are a few random memories from that time:

The Peabody at Memphis, Tennessee

One of the first great hotels that I visited was The Peabody Hotel in downtown Memphis. The hotel had originally opened in 1869 and soon became an important social hub, with Presidents Andrew Jackson and William McKinley as well as many Confederate generals among its guests. In 1923 the original hotel closed and reopened two years later in its current location on Union and 2nd Street.

The Peabody is undeniably a throwback to a flamboyant era, but it is not famous for its elegant guest rooms, its lavish ballrooms or even for the lobby bar which is packed every evening with the Memphis great and good. No, the Peabody Hotel is known for its ducks. In 1933 the General Manager of the hotel returned with some of his friends following a hunting trip, and the group thought that it would be a lark to let their call ducks (birds with particularly loud calls used by hunters as lures for wild ducks), to swim in the marble fountain in the hotel lobby, whilst the gents celebrated boisterously. The ducks unsurprisingly attracted a great deal of attention from other guests, and it was decided to keep five mallards in the hotel.

In 1940 one of the bellmen at the hotel took a special interest in the ducks and even trained them to walk in single file, once more attracting the interest of locals and visitors alike and soon the March of the Ducks became a twice daily occurrence. At eleven a.m. each morning a red carpet is rolled out from the elevators to the fountain and the crowds gather on either side. Souza's King Cotton March is played over the lobby's sound system and the elevator door opens to reveal the stars of the show who waddle and flap until they reach the cooling waters of the fountain. At five p.m. the performance is repeated, albeit in reverse, and the ducks retire for the night to their rooftop 'Duck Palace'.

The Peabody Ducks became national celebrities and featured on many TV shows – they even had their own sponsor in the shape of American Airlines who transported them around the country in the style to which they had become accustomed – and they are looked after by a designated member of the bell staff who is given the title 'The Duckmaster.' Over the years various celebrities have been invited to become an 'Honorary Duckmaster' assisting with the parade and on two occasions in the 1990s I was afforded that honour. I had to go to the roof of the hotel and help usher the ducks into the elevator and then wait with them until the moment came to take the journey to the lobby. As we neared the ground floor so we could hear the strains of Souza's march and as the doors opened, we were greeted by a huge crowd of camera-toting visitors who laughed and cheered and applauded as the avian superstars did their party piece. I have received many honours during my touring years but being a Duckmaster ranks high among them!

On my first visit to The Peabody I remember being introduced to the marketing director of the hotel and in an attempt to make conversation I mentioned that some friends of mine had stayed at The Peabody in Orlando and had thoroughly enjoyed the March of the Peabody Ducks there, to which I was given a withering gaze and told that 'We have the only Peabody ducks here in Memphis – those in Florida are wannabe ducks!'

In those days I used to perform three times a day – typically this would be at two tea events (one at eleven-thirty a.m. and one at three p.m., to allow for the duck marches) and then again during a dinner. I enjoyed the tea performances more because I didn't have to break the show up, it felt like a proper theatrical presentation. At The Peabody I performed in the Continental Ballroom, and the hotel erected a stage and provided bright theatre lights for me.

During one year's visit a photographer was detailed to get pictures of my show, and he was present at every performance I gave, so that by the end he knew exactly where he wanted to be, to capture the perfect shot with the perfect background with the perfect light and shadow. The result was an incredible collection of pictures which Caroline and I used for marketing for years to come.

Those early years could be tough, as Caroline had me running all over the place, and in 1999 I arrived at The Peabody at 12.45 a.m. on a Monday morning, having performed twice that day in Florida. Having fallen asleep, my alarm woke me again at four-thirty a.m., as I had to be in costume for a live TV interview at 5.15 p.m. and then performed three times throughout the day. My diary from that year makes difficult reading even now, as I was obviously exhausted and at the end of my tether, I wrote about one of The Peabody shows that 'I can tell, as soon as I start, that I have no energy left to give a good performance today. The timing is sluggish, the voice is strained, the movements badly timed.' Later in the day, at the second show I related that my performance was 'more tired than before. The voice more strained.' By the dinner show I was in a very bad place and could feel 'my throat tightening and my head aching as I try too hard to make up for my shortcomings.'

Despite that day, I now have only very happy memories of The Peabody and would love to return one day.

The St Paul Hotel, St Paul, Minnesota

Another favourite stopping place during my early tours was in the heart of the Minnesota capital of St Paul. The hotel stands on the edge of a park which was inevitably snow-covered and prettily lit for Christmas. Traditionally my visit was the last stop on my tours, and I would often get to stay there for three or four days, allowing me to unpack my suitcase for the first time in weeks. I would perform during the Christmas week at a series of tea events (The St Paul Hotel tried dinners, but they never really worked, for some reason. Maybe the extreme Minnesota cold kept people from going out in the evenings)

My performances at The St Paul where in a large ballroom, and a square stage was set up in the centre, with tea tables set on all sides, meaning that no guest was ever too far from the stage, but also meaning that I couldn't really focus my performance, needing to ensure that everyone had a little bit of me throughout the show. It was at St Paul that I first had the idea of leaving the stage and performing among the tables, using guests as part of the story. As I described Scrooge as a 'tight-fisted hand at the grindstone, a squeezing, wrenching, grasping, scraping, covetous old sinner…' I would weave my way between the tables and clap my hands on the shoulders of an older gentleman at the line's conclusion. Invariably his family would laugh, and I would ask 'Am I right? You can always tell, you can see it in their eyes!' Of course, I would return to the same gentleman at the end, so that he became the new Scrooge also. I would also find someone to be Fezziwig and maybe dance a little jig with them, while if there was a lady close to the stage who was firmly engaged by the action, she would become the ghost of Christmas Past – 'a strange creature…!' Topper would invariably find a suitably beautiful and demure younger lady to be the object of his flirtations

I used to spend time before the performance looking at the crowd as they arrived, trying to work out who I could pick on for each role. Not only was it important to choose people who would play along and not feel intimidated, but also to ensure that they were spread equally around the room, so that no quarter felt overlooked.

The interaction with the crowd was fun and brought people into the show, but eventually began to overwhelm the original text and become a distraction.

Because my shows in St Paul were in the last days before Christmas there was always a great atmosphere in the room as families dressed in their smartest Christmas sweaters and suits and exchanged gifts; laughter and conviviality filled the room. It was always a lovely way to finish my season and I had many old friends in St Paul who came to my show every year that I performed there.

When I stopped visiting St Paul, the management brought

a new show in to fill the same slot, and it was a staged radio presentation of 'It's a Wonderful Life'. I would very much like to see the performance sometime, and to sit in the ballroom wallowing in happy memories of running between the tables as people laughed and cheered.

The Hotel Hershey

Set on a hilltop overlooking the chocolate town of Hershey, the hotel of the same name is both elegant yet welcoming. Some of these hotels have a rather superior feel to them, as if only the very rich are permitted through their doors, but the Hotel Hershey is a true resort hotel where fun is to be had at every opportunity.

Hershey has remained on my schedule right up to my recent tours and I have always very much enjoyed visiting. From the moment you walk to the reception desk and are asked if you would like milk or plain chocolate to take to your room (well, it is Hershey, after all), you are welcomed as an old friend.

In the last years of the 19th century Milton Hershey forged a career in chocolate, he embraced his new trade learning how to make caramel too, before building both a chocolate and his own milk-processing plant in his hometown, not far from Harrisburg in Pennsylvania. Milton was a good and generous employer and the town grew and grew to both house and to entertain his loyal employees, even building them a theme park for their relaxation and enjoyment. During the depression years Hershey revealed plans to build an impressive hotel overlooking the factory and employed over eight hundred men to complete the project, bringing much needed work to the struggling community. The hotel opened in 1933 and has flourished ever since.

Although a beautiful hotel, staffed by amazing people, Hershey has always been a difficult venue for me to perform in. As with all of the hotels that Caroline booked for me, the shows were to be performed around meal services, and the locations chosen were two of the most theatrically inappropriate you can imagine! In a theatre or auditorium, the show is all, everything is focussed on the production on stage – the lights are focussed on the performer, the seats face the performer, the audience are there to see the performer, but in a hotel such as Hershey there is so much more to show off – not least the venue itself. For an afternoon tea I was asked to perform in The Fountain Lobby, which is an impressive area outside the main restaurant. The lobby is constructed of marble and is two stories high. At one end there are huge picture windows overlooking the town of Hershey and Hersheypark, and in the centre is the impressive fountain, which gives the lobby its name. For the tea service (featuring a lot of chocolate, of course) individual tables were laid all around the space, some hidden under the balcony at the edges, some close to the fountain, larger groups accommodated at each end of the room, meaning that at any given time about a quarter of the guests couldn't see what I was doing (and if there was a low sun setting, then anyone looking towards the great windows were rendered blind). There was no stage, no chair or hatstand, no focal point to the performance, I just had to keep moving, circling the room over and over, to make sure that everybody saw something, even though nobody saw everything.

At other venues I used the audience as part of the show, as I described in the St Paul Hotel passage, but at Hershey I couldn't even do that, for those on the other side of the room couldn't tell what was going on and would get distracted, so I just had to keep on moving: round and round and round: I christened it my Lighthouse Performance.

The second venue at Hershey was the Circular Dining Room, the signature restaurant at the hotel. When Milton Hershey had built the hotel he decreed that no guest should be sat in the corner, so the restaurant was built as a huge circle with views over the formal gardens to the rear. At the centre of the room was a large circular bar and the dining tables were laid out all around, meaning that The Lighthouse Show was called on once more for dinner.

At both shows I had the disconcerting experience of being watched by myself. The audio-visual team at the hotel had created a gobo (a sort of stencil for theatrical lights) based on a photograph of me in my top hat, and projected it onto the ceiling of both the lobby and the dining room. So as I twirled around below it was as if my presence was in the Heavens, as if Michelangelo had stopped in Pennsylvania on his way home from completing the Sistine Chapel!

But while the physical performing spaces may have been a challenge, my time at Hershey was always a delight – the staff became good friends (it is always the mark of a good hotel when the staff turnover is low and the same smiling faces greet the guests year after year), and the surroundings were incredible. Sometimes the gently rolling terrain would be covered with snow, and I would take the opportunity to rent a sled and revert to childhood once more, on other years there would be a warm sunshine bathing the countryside and I would play some golf at the nearby Hersey Golf Club. On one year I had a free day before driving onto my next venue, so took the chance to drive to Gettysburg where I walked through the famous battlefield, soaking up American history, and felt the waves of sorrow that I always feel at scenes of conflict.

It was not only the staff members who were familiar, but audience members came back year after year and in particular

Photo Credit: Author's Collection

young Derek, who attended from maybe the age of six with his grandparents. Derek was always smartly dressed, hair neatly combed, and he would offer a polite handshake and thank me for my performance. In later years it became a tradition for him to bring me a gift, and most memorable among them was a box of beer in honour of Dickens' description of Fezziwig's party: 'there was a great piece of Cold Roast, and there was a great piece of Cold Boiled, and there were mince-pies, and plenty of beer.' Possibly a strange gift from a six-year-old, but most imaginative and generous, nonetheless.

The Ojai Valley Inn and Spa

Some eighty-five miles to the northwest of Los Angeles airport, and nestling in a high valley is the sprawling complex that makes up one of the most relaxing hotels I have ever stayed at, The Ojai Valley Inn.

Ojai itself is a small town 745 feet above sea level and the valley is bordered to the north by the majestic Topatopa Mountains which take on a tinge of rose as the sun sets each evening, creating what the locals call 'The Pink Moment'.

Ojai was different to the other hotels that Caroline booked for me to perform at, as it wasn't in a downtown or an urban setting and necessitated a long drive to get there. The journey to the hotel was part of the joy of my appearances there. I would fly into LAX, slightly despairing at the sight of an apparently endless urban jungle, although getting childishly excited when I caught sight of the Hollywood sign on its hillside.

When I had eventually navigated the tangle of the airport and found my way to the car rental area, I would take a deep breath and set out onto the freeways of Los Angeles. Typically, I would arrive at around four p.m. and the roads – the busiest in America – would be bloated with rush-hour traffic. The very first time I drove in America was on these highways and I remember thinking, 'if I can survive here, then I can drive anywhere!' The route roughly followed the Pacific Ocean as far as Ventura, halfway between Los Angeles and Santa Barbara, and from there headed into the mountains.

The visit to Ojai came late in those early tours and I would be exhausted from almost six weeks on the road, of constant travel, of three performances a day, of flying in costume, of changing in McDonald's restrooms and now the drive took me higher and higher into the mountains and in my rear view mirror I could see that I was leaving the layer of yellow cloying smog, and the sprawl of the city behind and beneath me, as if I were sloughing off all of my stresses and strains. I would open the windows and breathe in the beautiful aroma of eucalyptus which filled the valley.

The sense of relaxion continued at the hotel as well, for Ojai only ever staged dinner events, no daytime teas, so I had plenty of time to relax and explore. Sometimes I would treat myself to a massage in the beautiful hotel spa, on one occasion the masseuse told me that I needed at least a week of treatment, so tight and tense were my muscles after the long trip. Other times I ventured out onto the golf course, with its astounding views, and one year I drove higher into the mountains and painted a small watercolour of the view before me, which for many years hung on my bathroom wall and reminded me of that very special place.

The dinners at Ojai had their own magic to them, as well. Whereas most of the hotels laid on very formal, silver service affairs, Ojai served the dinner 'family style'. All the guests were seated around circular tables of ten, randomly assigned as reservations were taken, rather than in smaller groups at individual tables, and when each course was served, large bowls and platters were brought to the table and everyone served themselves, or each other, and conversation flowed freely. As we dined a group of madrigal singers made their way around the room and sung old Christmas songs. The effect of the music was remarkable, for they surrounded each table, meaning that the perfectly arranged harmonies mingled and fell upon us as if each group of diners had its very own surround sound system.

The ballroom at Ojai was big, and the dinner was performed for around two hundred guests, but it always felt friendly and intimate.

One of the questions I am often asked is 'what is your favourite place to perform in?' Of course, the questioner inevitably wants me to cite their own city as the ultimate venue, but during the Caroline Jackson years I could quite honestly answer, 'Ojai'.

The Williamsburg Inn

If Ojai was the embodiment of relaxed pleasure, then The Williamsburg Inn oozed formality and class, and that statement is not meant in anyway to be a criticism of one of the most perfect hotels you could ever wish to stay in.

Colonial Williamsburg in Virginia is a town which was rescued from obscurity by Jon D Rockefeller in the 1920s and rebuilt to represent a genuine Revolutionary American city. In the mid-1700s, Williamsburg had been the capital of the Commonwealth of Virginia, so holds a very important place in American history. George Washington was a regular visitor, and it was in Williamsburg that many of the plans against the British were drawn up. When the town was rebuilt, it was to attract visitors, but it was never to be a kitsch theme-park. Modern day visitors would stroll around the streets as the population apparently went about their daily lives – tending their small patches of garden, cleaning their sparse houses, attending church, and selling their wares in the stores. All of the actors would be expert in the history of the day and would never break character. In fact, many is the time that I, as Brit, have felt somewhat uneasy being in the cradle of the Revolution, and have had a nagging suspicion that I should be telling someone in London about what I was hearing.

For a community built by one of the great American millionaires, it was necessary to have a hotel that would be appropriate for such classes and The Williamsburg Inn originally opened in 1937. Sitting a little way from The Duke of Gloucester Street, the main thoroughfare of the historical district, the Inn oozes Southern charm, it is two stories high with a porticoed entrance and a grand driveway circling around a reflecting pool, leading up to the main entrance. Once through the doors, which are opened by the ever-attendant bell staff, you walk into a spacious hallway, with views over the gardens to the rear, but this is no hotel reception lobby, no, for that would be far too gauche. In fact, the front desk is tucked away in a small room off the hallway, out of sight.

The main building of the hotel has been extended on a few occasions but has never lost its character, and no two suites are the same, each exquisitely appointed and furnished with antique furniture.

Such is the quality of the Williamsburg Inn that the Queen of England has stayed there on her two visits to the city, and I have occasionally been fortunate enough to have been given her suite of rooms during my stay there. In a blog post a few years ago I wrote:

'The suite is stunning. Entering from the corridor you find yourself in a little private hallway from where you continue into a lavishly appointed drawing room, where one can receive one's guests.

'I still can't believe it. There is the desk where the Queen sat to do her correspondence, here is a sofa on which she took tea and chatted. There is the bed in which she slept, the bath where she bathed, the basin where she brushed her teeth, the lavatory where… no, I think it may be treasonable to have such thoughts.'

The room in which I have always performed at the Inn is The Regency Room which for many years was the hotel's main restaurant. Tables were set around a dancefloor and at my back were views across the golf course. The restaurant was under the control of two amazing members of staff, Delphine and Leroy.

Leroy was a proud military man, short of stature but rigid in deportment. He ran the waiting staff as if they were a platoon on the field of battle and everyone respected and admired him, he was also one of the nicest people you could ever happen to meet. In charge of the front of house team was Delphine and, oh my word, you did not want to cross her! On one occasion Hollywood arrived at Williamsburg and the actor Colin Farrel was staying at the hotel. Farrel is known as one of Hollywood's hellraisers, getting anything that he wants on set by dint of exploding into major tantrums. One morning during filming he arrived at the Regency Room for breakfast without socks on and Delphine sent him packing: 'You do NOT come into my restaurant improperly dressed! You go back to your room and you dress correctly and THEN I will let you come in!' And sure enough he slunk back to his suite tail firmly between his legs. Fortunately, during my years at Williamsburg, I never crossed Delphine.

As with all of Caroline's hotel bookings my show was based around a superb dinner and the kitchens at Williamsburg liked to offer the full, formal, five-course dinner experience, meaning that the events didn't finish until very late at night. In general at such events I would be sat at one of the dining tables, often with important sponsors or members of a board, meaning that I would be called upon to keep up an entertaining banter even when I was not actually performing, which made the dinner theatre shows very tiring indeed.

I remember one year, when the hotel had undergone a complete renovation to ensure that the grandeur was not faded but genuine, a capacity audience gathered in the Regency Room – there must have been around 150 of us – and everyone was in high spirits, when suddenly the fire alarms sounded. As part of the modernisation works a new system had been installed and it was over-sensitive having not been correctly calibrated. There was nothing to do but dutifully make our way outside until the staff investigated the cause of the alarm. Unfortunately, that night it was raining very hard and we all had to gather under the awning that covered the red carpet in front of the main door. I seem to remember that we sang a few carols until we were allowed to resume our seats and the show could continue.

The dinners at Williamsburg were always elegant affairs, with many guests in dinner jackets and ball gowns, but the hotel also staged tea events too and this attracted a different audience with many in colourful Christmas sweaters. The guests would take their seats and be served tea, sandwiches and cakes and when all was ready I would start my performance, which was rather easier than the dinner format because I could run straight through, except for the fact that Leroy asked if I could pause in the middle, so that teacups could be replenished (what a splendidly British dilemma), so at the point when Scrooge has ridded himself of The Ghost of Christmas Past and slumped into his chair, I would add to Dickens' original narrative '... and fell into a deep sleep and dreamed of fresh cups of tea, plates of cakes and the interval…'

One of the greatest pleasures of travelling to Williamsburg was meeting up with my old friend Ryan Fletcher and his wife Jeannie. Ryan is a trained opera singer and lectures at William and Mary College, one of the top educational establishments in America, as well as enjoying a professional performing career. For many years Ryan also worked for the Colonial Williamsburg Foundation, playing Mr Greenhaugh in one of the stores on The Duke of Gloucester Street, regaling the visitors with his perfectly prepared spiel, and witty improvisation. Ryan was booked by the Inn to give my introductions and we soon formed a close friendship, borne out of our shared experiences of life on the road.

Ryan and Jeannie also got on very well with my wife Liz, who in more recent years often joined me at the end of my tours. Before we adopted our two daughters, my trips would be longer than they are now, and after Liz's teaching commitments in the UK were over, she would fly to America and often our reunions would be in Williamsburg meaning that it is a venue of which we can share memories.

Often attached to my visits to Williamsburg was a stop in the small town of Occoquan, a suburb of Washington DC. My event sponsor was a small Christmas gift shop called The Golden Goose which was packed with every description of seasonal ornaments that you could imagine. I would arrive at the store and make my way to the front of a long queue and would sit for an hour or so signing books and gifts. When the first signing session was done, we all (I and the audience) walked along the main street of the town to a tiny chapel where I would perform my show, and then we all walked back to the store for another signing session. I made many friends at The

Golden Goose both among the staff and the customers and it was with great sadness that I received the news just a year or so ago that Pat and Laverne, the shop's owners, had decided to retire and close the store for good, meaning that I would never be able to perform there again. Wonderfully, the name of the chapel in which I performed was 'The Ebenezer Chapel' which gave me the opportunity to adlib slightly: at the moment old Scrooge is celebrating on Christmas morning Dickens tells us that he 'went to Church', so I made sure that on that line I was in the central aisle and could walk reverently towards the alter and kneel, before turning my head to the audience and whispering to them —'look, they even named the church after me!'

There were many other venues as well, but those grand hotels were the ones that I returned to year after year, and in the case of Hershey and Williamsburg still perform at today, and were the venues that formed the bedrock of my early performing career in America.

Chapter 4
The Tour Grows, Develops and Changes Forever

The contract with the Historic Hotels of America had a double benefit, not only did it allow Caroline to fill my tour with lucrative dates, it also brought me to the attention of a lot of people many of whom came from other organisations or communities and who saw the possibility of my visiting them also.

Caroline took calls from libraries, societies, and small festivals and soon the tour was growing to six or seven weeks. Generally, the weekend dates were spent at the hotels, whilst the rest of the time I was flying and driving all over the place. At this time the tour made little coherent logistical sense, and I may be travelling from east to west, or north to south and back again in the matter of a few days. Often there was little time to prepare for a show and I would have to sit on an aircraft in full costume, so that we could drive to a venue as soon as we 'deplaned' (a verb that I learned during that time). Sometimes if I wasn't in costume, we would have to stop at a fast-food restaurant and I would change in the less than salubrious surroundings of a restroom, before arriving at the next venue. If we were driving, then I would often be squashed in the back seat, hemmed in by cartons of 'Christmas With Dickens' books as well as the other merchandise that Caroline offered for sale. In those days before smart phones or satellite navigation systems, we often got lost, so many where the times that I arrived for a show late, flustered and woefully under-prepared. In fact, often being on stage was the most peaceful and calm moment of the day.

One new venue that came to us very early on was at Fayetteville, a small town in southern Tennessee which staged a winter festival called 'The Host of Christmas Past'. The idea was to promote the town's Victorian era downtown region, and to bring business to the stores and milk bars that had been there for a hundred years or more. The festival was run by the local Chamber of Commerce and more particularly by an energetic and resourceful lady, Marie Caldwell.

In my diaries of the time I described Fayetteville as being like the town in 'Back to the Future', in that everything was built around an old courthouse which stood proudly in the centre of the square. Various statues to soldiers who had fought in the Civil War stood silently protecting the old building and there was always a great sense of pride to the town.

The festival would open with the singing of the National Anthem, which would be performed by a fine tenor singer, one of Fayetteville's great success stories. He would sing unaccompanied and the whole square would fall into silence, as everyone stood with the hands over their hearts – it was always a profoundly moving moment. In the midst of loud, brash, corporate America, was this very genuine display of national pride.

At Fayetteville I would typically perform a couple of times, maybe in a high school, or a small theatre, and on occasion in the Court House itself, but it was the meet and greet sessions that Marie really promoted. Various businesses would sign up to host me, and I would walk into whichever store and sit at a table. Marie brought a large printed notice with us that had a photograph of me, and the words: 'GERALD CHARLES DICKENS. SIGNING HERE' (Marie, like the true southerner she was, always called me Gerald Charles). As all of the businesses were situated around the square, it was natural that as the day wore on the amount of visitors to my little signing table diminished. One year at the tail-end of the afternoon Marie and I were in a gift shop and as there was nobody coming in we were chatting about this and that, when an older lady shuffled through the door and stood in front of my desk. I said 'Hello', but she didn't answer. She peered myopically at me, and then at the sign, and then at me again, still without speaking. This seemed a slightly awkward situation, until she suddenly said, in a husky voice and with a very broad Tennessee accent, 'Well! You gonna sing?'

'I'm sorry?' I replied, not sure if I had heard her correctly.

'Are you gonna sing?'

Marie stepped in to assist, 'No, he aint gonna sing, this is Gerald Charles Dickens!'

The lady peered at the notice again before continuing 'It SAYS he's gonna sing! Are you kin to Little Jimmy Dickens?' At this point Marie became helpless with laughter, for not only had the lady misread 'sign' for 'sing' but also had connected me with one of America's top country stars, rather than a dead British author.

Eventually Marie recovered and said 'No, he aint related to Little Jimmy, he is a great-great-grandson to Charles Dickens, who wrote 'A Christmas Carol.' The lady looked closely at me again, then turned on her heel, saying as she left the shop 'Nope! Not never heard of him!'

Fayetteville also played a small part in changing my show forever. Marie had asked me to perform for some members of the Chamber of Commerce as well as other notable townsfolk.

I was to talk about 'Dickens the Entrepreneur' and then read the final chapter from my show. The event was in a fairly sterile meeting room in a fairy sterile Holiday Inn, situated on the edge of the town. I, of course, was in Victorian costume and the reaction was positive, if not totally. I laid my book down and took my bows, but there was no time to linger and chat, for I had a second appearance of the day in Maddison, Alabama, an hour to the south. Time was tight and there was no opportunity to change so I jumped into Caroline's car in full costume waving my farewells as we left Fayetteville. Caroline got a bit lost, as was often the case, meaning that when we arrived at the library the scheduled time for my performance had come and gone and the audience was patiently waiting for me. They had nothing to look at but a lectern.

Eventually we pulled up and it was indeed fortunate that I was in costume for it meant that I could start my reading without further delay. But now a sudden horror flashed through my mind as I took in the situation: my reading script lay on the lectern, but unfortunately the lectern in question was not the one in Madison but the one an hour to the north in the Holiday Inn on the outskirts of Fayetteville.

I felt helpless and naked and very scared. The audience sat looking at me and I stood looking at them - now what? And it was then that a ridiculous thought came to my mind. I had been performing this story for a few years now, was it possible that I could recite it from memory? I knew it began 'Marley was dead, to begin with.' I knew it ended 'God bless us, every one!' I knew that four ghosts appeared, and that Scrooge started mean and ended nice. I may, just may, be able to pull this off. If anyone complained that I wasn't using the correct text, I could always claim that this was a little-known early draft of the story that only the Dickens family had access to. I decided to give it a go.

95

I walked up to the lectern and began: 'Marley was dead, to begin with…' at which point my mind went blank, this wasn't a promising start, but then the next line came to me, 'there was no doubt of that. The register of his burial was signed by the clergyman, the clerk, the undertaker and the chief mourner.' And so it continued! I discovered that thanks to my many performances I roughly knew the entire script by heart. It soon became apparent that there was no need to stand at an empty lectern, so I moved it out of the way and instead starting moving other furniture, which lay about the room, to use in the performance: a chair represented Scrooge's counting house and then doubled up as his bed. A stool became Bob Cratchit's seat in the office but would prove perfect to also represent Tiny Tim's seat at the Christmas table.

As the show continued I found myself working on two levels of consciousness - one was centred on giving the best performance I could, so was focussed on the lines and emotions that I had worked on, whilst the other was on a more practical plane, almost as if I were looking down at myself from above, planning where I needed to be and what furniture and props I could use to enhance the words. It was certainly an exhilarating and exciting evening.

When the show came to an end the audience applauded loudly and I knew that my professional life had just changed forever. As I prepared to leave the library a lady came up to me to offer her congratulations: 'Mr Dickens,' she said, 'That was very enjoyable, we thought you were going to be giving us a reading, we didn't expect it to be memorised!' 'That's a coincidence,' I thought 'neither did I!' She continued to talk, 'And to perform like that with your medical condition was truly inspiring.' This latter comment was a surprise to me for I was feeling in good health, and I told her so. 'I understand that you may not want to talk about it and that is understandable, but I work as a nurse and I could tell.' My confusion increased and I asked her to explain and soon the reason for her suspicions became clear. When I had been performing on automatic pilot I had just let my standard show do the work, which meant that all of my gestures were being given by my right hand only, as had aways been the case when I was reading - she was convinced that I was recovering from a stroke and had suffered a left-side paralysis.

That evening in Maddison was one of the most important shows that I have ever given and from that day on I never performed another 'reading' of *A Christmas Carol.*

My happy times in Fayetteville came back to me last year, when I received the sad news from Marie's family that she had died peacefully in her beloved hometown for which she had done so much to promote.

Reading in Fayetteville City Halls
Photo Credit: Author's Collection

Chapter 5
Memories from the Early Tours

Claymont, Delaware

Within a very few years the 'Annual Holiday Tour' had grown into a huge operation. I would be away for seven, sometimes eight weeks, at a time and would be travelling all over the country. I had bookings in California, and Boston; Wisconsin and Alabama, Washington State and Georgia, and almost every day I was on the road, travelling. Having been a naive traveller I soon became an expert one and took great delight in manoeuvring myself during the boarding process so that I was at the front of whichever group I was in and could get a good chance of finding an overhead bin. It was often necessary to travel in costume, as I have mentioned before, and I would get strange looks from my fellow passengers as I stowed my top hat box. On one occasion I was flying to Wilmington, Delaware, where I was due to perform on behalf of the Darley Society. Felix Darley was an American artist and supplied illustrations to some American editions of Dickens' works, he lived in the small town of Claymont, not far from Wilmington, and when Charles Dickens toured with his readings in 1867/8, Darley offered his house to stay in, away from the bustle and crowds of the city. The Darley House was an oasis for the great man, where he could relax.

By the time I was following in the footsteps of Charles Dickens, the Darley House had been bought by an ebullient and larger than life character by the name of Ray Hester. Ray ran the house as a B&B, but also wanted to share his great knowledge of Felix and to this end was instrumental in forming the society in the artists' name. When Ray heard about my tours, he contacted Caroline and started to make arrangements for a visit there. The house itself was too small to stage an event in, but I was to stay there, in the same room as my great-great-grandfather had a hundred and some years before.

Sometimes organisers of smaller events feel that they cannot supply the glitz and the glamour of better funded, more corporate shows, so tend to go out of their way to make things special and memorable for me in different ways, and Ray certainly didn't stint in his efforts. In those days, and this was pre 9-11, people could gather at an arrival gate in the airport to meet an incoming flight, and on that occasion as I rather blearily left the plane I was greeted by the entire Darley Society dressed in Victorian costumes serenading me with 'We Welcome you Mr Dickens, We Welcome You Mr Dickens, We Welcome You Mr Dickens to the state of Del-Ware! To the tune of 'We Wish You a Merry Christmas'. My fellow passengers were somewhat surprised to be welcomed in this manner, and I felt quite embarrassed by the whole affair, but it was a wonderful gesture. The team had also booked a huge stretch limousine, which was waiting for us outside the baggage claim doors and whisked us all away as if I were some major VIP: it was very grand!

The shows for the Darley Society were always well attended, and organised with Ray's typical ebullience and flair, and after they had finished I would return to the grand old house where Dickens himself had rested.

Springfield, Illinois

Another airport-related anecdote came in 2001, in the aftermath of the 9-11 terrorist attacks. I had thought long and hard as to whether I should travel to America at all that winter, for the threat of further attacks was still very real. Caroline put no pressure on me, even though she had so much invested in the annual tour, but let me come to my own decision, which, in the end, was to travel. Throughout that tour I wore a small Stars and Stripes pin in my lapel at every show, to show solidarity for America, and it became one of my most memorable trips, for the audiences were in desperate need of entertainment, and to be reassured by the simplicity of a bygone era.

But even out of that dark time, humour arose. As ever I was flying all over the place and of course the restrictions and security measures had been elevated. Even for a domestic flight it was suggested that passengers should arrive at airports three hours before the scheduled departure time. I had been performing in Springfield Illinois, and my onward flight was due to depart at eight a.m., meaning I was required to check in at five a.m. Cars were not allowed to drive up to the terminal building, and passengers had to be dropped off a good distance away, so I had to drag my baggage up to the main building, which I found to be locked. A kindly gentleman responded to my beating on the door and Springfield Airport was opened for me.

Inside, the same gentleman took up a position behind a counter and started checking me in. 'Tap,' went the keyboard. 'Tap, tap tappptappptaptap…' He stopped and peered at the screen, then at me and back to the screen again. 'Sir, you have been selected for a random security check.' How random was that? I was the only passenger in the airport! 'Please take your case to the table over there, sir.' So, the same man -the janitor and desk clerk - now became chief security officer also and having asked me to open my case (the lid lifting towards me, so that I could not see inside), began to peer into my belongings. It seemed to be a thorough search and after a while he called for a colleague to join him: 'here, take a look at this', he said. The lady in question peered into my case, nodded, and the two exchanged a brief glance, while they whispered. What was going on? What had they found in my luggage? Had something been planted there? A further call went out and this time the member of the Illinois National Guard who was patrolling the airport (he looked as if were about fifteen, and as if he would open fire if anyone even sneezed) came over and joined his friends, so that now three officials were scrutinising my belongings. I was feeling rather hot and a little uneasy, 'Um, is everything all right?' I asked somewhat nervously. 'Oh, yes!' replied the original gentleman, 'We were just commenting that we have rarely seen such a neatly packed suitcase. Have a great day!'

Later on in that tour, 2001, I was performing at a small arts centre on Staten Island and before I went to the venue, I was given a brief driving tour which took me down to the shore. I looked across to Manhattan and for the first time saw the incomplete skyline. A wave of sadness and sorrow came over me as I thought of what I would have seen had I been on the same spot two months before. I wore my American flag pin with great pride that year.

The Largest and Smallest Audiences
A question I am often asked, particularly by people interested in booking me for their own venue, is 'what is the average size of your audiences?' And the only reply that I can give is to tell them the smallest and the largest – then they can find an

101

average.

The largest crowd I ever played to was, inevitably, in Texas. Caroline had pulled off a real coup by signing a contract with a large Dallas-based software company for me to be the entertainment at their annual staff Christmas party. Not only would I be performing during dinner, but every guest would be presented with a signed leather A Christmas Carol bookmark as a token of their employer's generosity.

This, as I said, was in Texas: things are big in Texas. There would be 2,000 guests at the dinner.

In order to get all 2,000 bookmarks signed Caroline had booked a motel room earlier in the tour close to where she lived in Arlington, Virginia, and for two or three days I sat in that small space scrawling 'Gerald Charles Dickens' over and over again. Sometimes it was Grld ChsD, sometimes Charles Gerald Charles Dickens, sometimes it bore no form at all. Caroline made occasional appearances to remove completed boxes, only to replace them with others - it seemed to take forever.

The event in Dallas came somewhere towards the end of the trip so after I had signed the bookmarks I was on the road as usual but always hovering in the background was the prospect of performing for 2000 people. Eventually the great day arrived and before we went to the hotel where the dinner was to be held, the senior board members of the company hosted an exclusive meet and greet session over lunch - at Southfork Ranch! The CEO gave a speech during which he welcomed me in a typically Texan style and presented me with a souvenir Stetson. As he ended his remarks he signed off with a flourish declaring 'Happy Yule Y'all!; I was sure that he was trying this line out on us, and having received a loud laugh I assumed that it would make a re-appearance at the evening's event.

After lunch we drove to the hotel and for the first time I saw what 2000 seats looked like, the tables were already set with linen, silver and crystal and seemed to spread as far as the eye could see. It was quite a terrifying moment. In pride of place at every setting lay a copy of *A Christmas Carol* complete with the signed bookmark. It was with a sigh of relief that I thought that I wouldn't have to do a signing session after the show that night - the hours in the Arlington motel would pay off now, I could just perform and leave.

The huge ballroom had a stage along one wall, where I would be performing, and I climbed up to try and get an idea of what I would be dealing with.

The room was very wide but not very deep and I was very aware that those people sitting at the far extremities of the room would struggle to see me. The organisers had thought of this and had mounted two huge screens on each side of the stage and a video camera immediately in front of me. The audio-visual equipment was handled by a professional company, and we spent a long time doing effective sound checks to make sure nothing was left to chance. When all the preparations were complete, I went up to my room until it was time for dinner.

When I returned, the ballroom was packed and noisy. Everyone was dressed in ridiculously expensive suits and dresses. Diamonds glistened, huge Rolex watches were conspicuously displayed. Hair, perfume, aftershave and make-up were perfect and cosmetic surgery of varying degrees was on bountiful display. Quite how everyone was called to order I don't remember, but everyone dutifully took their seats and were welcomed by the CEO who sure enough wished everyone 'Happy Yule Ya'll' and then he handed over to me to begin my first performance. It was a fascinating exercise for me: at first I wanted to be as inclusive as I could, so was making a real effort to perform to the very far extremities of the room, but in doing this I glanced the images of myself on the big screens and realised that the camera was only getting my profile and any facial expressions that I was making were completely lost. Therefore, when I returned for the second and subsequent chapters I began to concentrate on the camera in front of me, and from being a HUGE performance it became a very small, intimate one. Ignoring seventy per cent of the room seemed counter intuitive to me, but in doing so I was giving those folks a much more complete show as they watched the screens.

Much wine and many cocktails were consumed that night and by the time I got to Tiny Tim's death scene there was much emotion in the room, and some high spirited, or highly spirited, revellers stood at the back and gently waved their cigarette lighters in the air as if they were at a rock concert. It was very late, maybe midnight, when the dinner finally ended and I took the applause. I had finished for the night and was looking forward to getting back to the solitude of my room, until the CEO returned to the stage and announced, 'You will see that you all a copy of *A Christmas Carol* on your table and I am sure that if you want them personalised Gerald Charles will be happy to facilitate that.' And so the night was extended as a large proportion of the group gathered around me asking for books to be inscribed to 'Jason J Jackson III' or 'Mary Lou' or 'Grandma and Gramps'. Some wanted me to write passionate declarations of love for a fiancé or significant other (dad had warned me of this in his treatise on signing written in '93), whilst others managed to grab whole piles of apparently ignored, forgotten and abandoned books and wanted me to sign them all. It was a very long night.

In contrast to that huge night, the smallest crowd I ever played to was during the same period, and was in Collierville, a small town just to the north of Memphis.

For a period of five years or so I attended a festival in the town, called Dickens on the Square. It was a lovely event, not dissimilar to the Host of Christmas Past in Fayetteville with lots of music and costumed characters entertaining the crowds. I performed A Christmas Carol in a small converted Church sanctuary, but it was another of my other regular shows that drew my miniature audience.

'A Child's Journey with Dickens' is a charming account of a meeting in a railroad car between Charles Dickens and a ten-year-old girl. In 1868 Dickens was travelling through New England giving readings in cities along the way and one such event was in Portland, Maine. On the morning after the performance he boarded a train to take him back to Boston and his base in The Parker House Hotel; on the same train sat a girl named Kate, who was one of his most ardent fans.

With the natural curiosity of a ten-year-old, Kate hid in the corner of Dickens' carriage so that she could watch him throughout the journey, and when he was for a moment alone, she emerged from her hiding place and took a seat beside him. He was understandably surprised, but her natural enthusiasm and honesty delighted him and soon they chatted as if they were the oldest and dearest of friends. She asked him which was his favourite book (David Copperfield, he told her) and she caused him to laugh aloud when she explained that she had read all of his books, although she did skip the 'very dull parts' once in a while. She compounded the insult by adding, 'Oh, not the short dull parts, just the long ones!'

Kate, the little girl in question, grew to become an author

in her own right and, as Kate Douglas Wiggin, famously wrote Rebecca of Sunnybrook Farm. In 1912 Kate was asked to give a speech in New York City remembering her day with Dickens and so popular was the presentation that she published the text and called it 'A Child's Journey with Dickens'.

In Collierville there is an historic train at the southern edge of the square and the cars are used for dining and entertaining. The idea came to the organisers of the festival that a railroad car would be a perfect setting for a performance of A Child's Journey with Dickens, and plans were laid. Usually when I perform the piece it is, of course, a one man show, meaning that I take the roles of Kate as an older woman reminiscing, Kate as an excitable ten-year old meeting her hero, and Charles Dickens himself. But in Collierville a new idea was presented to me, that being that I should perform alongside a younger girl. The Dickens on the Square Event was organised by Donna Bartz, and her daughter Jessica was keen on theatre with ambitions to go into the profession. Donna asked if it would be possible to re-work the script using Jessica as the young Kate, whilst I continued to narrate and play Dickens. During whichever tour it was, I don't recall the exact year, I sent the new script to Jessica and she worked on it on her own, but we only met for the first time on the day of the performance itself. We rehearsed as much as my tight timetable allowed until evening came and it was time to perform. The audience squeezed onto the railroad car we performed to around twenty people I would guess. I think we performed for two or three different sittings, and the show got better and better as we learned how to work together. Jessica and I repeated the performance in various other locations during subsequent years until she left for college, but those first performances in an American railroad car will always hold special memories for me.

Waynesville, Ohio

On one occasion I was invited to perform in the little town of Waynesville, Ohio, which is not far from Cincinnati. The event organisers had got in touch with Caroline because Charles Dickens had passed through the town during his 1842 trip and had not been favourably impressed. He was staying at The Golden Lamb hotel in nearby Lebanon, and in his travel book American Notes he wrote: 'We dine soon afterwards with the boarders in the house and have nothing to drink but tea and coffee. As they are both very bad and the water is worse, I ask for brandy; but it is a Temperance Hotel, and spirits are not to be had for love or money.' Leaving Lebanon, his thirst unquenched, Dickens then stopped in Waynesville where he asked at a simple inn for brandy, but received the same response as before. Local legend has it that Dickens strode down the main street to another inn and requested brandy there but discovered that was also a temperance house. Frustrated he boarded his carriage and left the town thumbing his nose at the residents.

When I visited the area, the locals were keen to make amends for my ancestor's frustrations. I was first taken to the Golden Lamb where, with great pride, the townsfolk poured me a huge glass of brandy and toasted me well. After a brief lunch we all drove to Waynesville where I was given more brandy at the sites of the two former inns, and there was even a small novelty decanter, in the shape of Mr Pickwick, filled to the brim with liquor in my hotel room. By the time I was due to step on stage later that evening there seemed to be two, if not three, of everything, and I am sure I grinned foolishly throughout the entire show.

But that visit to Ohio also allowed me to introduce a new aspect to my performance, for my hosts owned a small antique store and presented me with a smart wooden walking cane as a token of their thanks. The cane dated back to the Victorian era, and I promised them that I would use it in my show. I duly strode onto the stage with it, before placing it at the back of the stage so that I could continue unhindered. It is (for I still have it) a simple cane with the handle forming the shape of a capital T, and as I reached the scene in the Cratchit's house I noticed it resting against a table looking for all the world like Tiny Tim's crutch, and from that day on I have always connected Scrooge to Tiny Tim via a simple wooden walking stick. So much of my performance has come from improvisation and coincidence and my time in Waynesville was another example of good fortune.

Aspen, Colorado

An experiment that Caroline never repeated was a trip to Aspen, Colorado one December, to perform in yet another grand hotel, The Jerome.

Caroline and I had flown together from the east coast to Denver where we were to connect with a local flight to Aspen, although for some reason we were not booked on the same plane, Caroline's leaving twenty minutes after mine. I duly arrived in the famous ski resort and was met by a representative of the hotel, and we waited for Caroline's flight to arrive. However, in that twenty-minute period the weather had closed in, and the second flight was forced to turn back. Caroline had settled herself in her seat and dozed off, waking only as she became aware of the plane making its final descent and was dismayed to notice that the sign on the airport terminal read 'DENVER'. I was on my own.

With the possibility of bad weather affecting our plans Caroline had arranged for us to fly with an entire day free, and so it was that while she was in a Denver airport hotel room, I had the luxury of a day in the mountains. I had been met by the Public Relations manager of the hotel and as we discussed what I could do with my unexpected vacation day she most naturally asked me 'do you ski?' I was in Aspen, what was I going to say? 'Oh, yes.' I confidently replied. 'Austria. The Alps.' Strictly speaking this was true, I had indeed skied in Austria a few years before, but what I failed to mention was that I had spent most of that week on my bottom, the only English student in an otherwise all German class, trying to understand a German-speaking instructor. My Alpine education based purely on watching everybody else carry out whatever the exercise was, then trying to mimic it . On one morning I had wiped out my entire class as my efforts to affect a snow plough stop failed spectacularly. I certainly wasn't the experienced skier that I might have implied.

The kindly PR director, no doubt having visions of press coverage of Mr Dickens schussing this way and that with great plumes of glistening powder in his wake, immediately took me to the ski shop and asked the staff to fit me up with boots, skis, and all the equipment. I tried on various boots until we found a pair that fitted, and the staff adjusted the bindings to match. I chose salopettes, gloves and a hat, and then, while various forms were filled and signed, I decided to try my boots again. I clipped them on and bent my knees making imaginary turns, at which point a rather nervous PR director looked over her shoulder at me and asked, 'are those boots comfortable?'

'Oh, yes,' I replied, 'they are perfect!'

'They may be even more comfortable if they were on the correct feet...' I could see a look of fear on her face that the hotel's investment in me was about to be completely wasted as she sent me up into the high peaks.

I did ski the next day, with a local guide, and although it wasn't pretty, I did make it back to the hotel intact. And the wonderful coincidence was that one of the main runs in Aspen is 'Little Nell', named after the character in Charles Dickens' The Old Curiosity Shop. Caroline never made it to Aspen, and after that near miss I never returned, either.

Reading my old diaries from those early tours I am amazed that I survived at all! Most days had two or three performances in, and any rest days were filled with travel. I was constantly waking up to 4am alarm calls, travelling in costume and travelling straight to performances: there was no down time or preparation time. Many of the entries talk about suffering from lack of energy and my throat tightening so that I couldn't project or enunciate effectively. The geography of the tours was a bit wild too, and I would fly from the east coast to the west, back to the south and then to the mid-west, there was no sense of coherence to the planning. However, I was living my dream and loving the opportunity to perform, as well as enjoying the adulation of the audiences: the lifeblood of an actor.

Caroline was certainly a hard taskmaster, but she opened up all sorts of avenues to me and introduced me to so many people. She was amazing in her communication skills and never forgot the family or details of people we met along the way, meaning that when we returned to a venue she was instantly enquiring about significant others, children or pets by name. I am terrible at remembering names and I learned so much by watching Caroline at work.

Prior to 9-11 my visas were granted for extended periods, and with each successive application the USA government seemed to feel safer with my presence, meaning that I was eventually granted my P-3 status for a five-year term. Caroline immediately offered me a contract for the same length, and we settled into a long stretch working together. During that final five-year stint I began to find things much harder, and I made up my mind to retire from touring at the end of the 2005 trip.

Many of the venues during that last year laid on special ceremonies for me, and whenever my introduction was made and the audiences were told that this would be my final appearance, there would be a gasp of disappointment. In a way the 2005 trip was difficult – Caroline and I were not close by then, despite having worked together for so long, and the atmosphere in the camp was chilly, to say the least, and then at every post-show signing session I had to answer all sorts of questions about my reasons for not returning in 2006. Many audience members and some venues regarded my retirement as a slight against them and even against America. It was a huge relief to reach St Paul, Minnesota and to leave the stage for the final time on the evening of 23 December.

My days of touring America were over, or so I thought.

Chapter 6
Back in Britain

Although I had been having great adventures in America, I was also performing in Britain too and as many of the venues were repeat bookings (such as the annual Rochester Dickens Festival), I had to introduce new scripts into my repertoire. Initially I concentrated on the readings that Charles had given himself, some of which I performed in the style that he had used, whilst others I developed into memorised scripts.

For the former style of events, I wanted to use a replica of the reading desk that Charles Dickens had designed for his performances. Fortunately, the Charles Dickens Museum had one that they used for events at 48 Doughty Street and allowed me to borrow it whenever I needed it. This was a very kind offer, especially as they didn't charge me anything, but it did entail driving into the centre of London to pick it up before every show. Eventually this became tiresome, but the museum came to help again by offering me an old desk that had been made for a television documentary many years before. It had been stored in a cupboard and was moth-eaten, but I was welcome to it, if I wanted it. I found a local upholsterer who was willing to cover it in red fabric, with golden trimmings, and a local carpenter who constructed the little shelf that Dickens used and I have been using that desk ever since.

Those early readings were based on Charles' own repertoire, and particularly Sikes and Nancy, the brutal murder scene from *Oliver Twist*, which even today I present in the traditional style. When Dickens performed 'The Murder' he would delight when ladies in the audience fainted, and on one occasion wrote a gleeful letter home to his family stating that 'between fifteen and twenty women were carried out quite stiff!'

When I first read the script of Sikes and Nancy (and 'script' is the correct term for it, for Dickens didn't simply read a passage from a novel, he carefully created a piece of theatre pulling passages from many different parts of the original), I was a little underwhelmed. Most of the reading is taken up by the character of Noah Claypole eavesdropping on Nancy and then telling old Fagin what he heard. The actual shocking murder takes only a line or two, and then the plot concentrates on Sike's escape and eventual death. What I hadn't appreciated was the anticipation that he had written into the script, with the tension gradually building like a psychological thriller. By the time that Sikes makes the fatal blow it is as if a high-pressure boiler is ready to blow and suddenly the tension in my body is released.

Sikes and Nancy
Photo Credit: Lewis J Brockway

Sikes and Nancy is a short reading compared to some others in the repertoire, but it is still one of the most exhausting and I can quite understand how it affected Dickens's health in the last years of his life.

Some of my new shows were very successful and are still part of my programme today, and some were too clever for their own good and have since faded into obscurity, but the creation of each brought me closer to Charles and gave me a better understanding of his character.

As ever my father was there with advice, and one performance he was desperate for me to give was a piece called Doctor Marigold, which I had never heard of. He talked about the fast 'patter' section and how it would suit my style. I didn't think that an obscure piece of Dickens was very suitable for a modern audience, and declined to read it, thinking that I knew best.

Instead, I concentrated on creating shows based on material that I knew: I have already spoken about Mr Dickens is Coming, and the next script I developed was Nicholas Nickleby. I wanted to capture the excitement that I had felt when I had watched the Royal Shakespeare Company's epic production, and the script was quite a romp through the skeleton of the story. I start the performance with an introduction admitting that I am unashamedly paying homage to the RSC, before pointing out that they had a cast of forty, and took eight hours to tell the story, whereas I have me and only 1 hour. Having invited the audience to bear with me and keep up (assuring that they become invested in the success of the show), I begin the script with the opening lines of the novel. There are rapid changes of character sharing rat-tat-tat conversations, with changes of voices and facial expressions being a major feature. I even manage to include a carefully scripted 'ad lib' when one character drops a prop, and the other, with whom he is engaged in conversation, breaks from the lines and asks his companion if he isn't going to pick up the errant article, there follows a moment of 'corpsing' before the two resume their characters.

Nicholas Nickleby has always been a popular choice and I have performed it in a wide variety of venues over the years.

'The Complete Works of Charles Dickens' was a show that I immensely enjoyed writing and I was very proud of the script, but it never really found a permanent place in my repertoire as it needed quite a deep knowledge of the works of Dickens to appreciate. The inspiration for the script came from an old theatrical anecdote: a young actor had produced and directed himself in a new show and had invited the great Noel Coward to come and see it on the opening night. After the final curtain Coward went to see the performer in his dressing room, and the young man, faced by this theatrical great, became somewhat awkward and tongue-tied. He couldn't think what to say, eventually deciding to concentrate on the technicalities and practicalities of the performance. He had been nervous about his costume and make up, so asked Coward, 'Could you see my wig join?' to which the reply was 'Perfectly, dear boy, perfectly!

The idea behind The Complete Works was to deliver a single narrative using passages from every one of Dicken's novels, in order, woven together in such a way that it would be impossible for an audience to 'see the join'. For example, the link between Our Mutual Friend and *The Mystery of Edwin Drood* uses two scenes featuring a river:

'After a darkening hour or so suddenly the rudder-lines tightened in his hold, and he steered towards the Surrey shore. Always watching his face, the girl instantly answered to the action in her sculling; presently the boat swung round, quivered as from a sudden jerk, and the upper half of the man was stretched out over the stern. *He got closer to the weir, and peered at its well-known posts and timbers. Nothing unusual was remotely shadowed forth. But he resolved that he would come back early in the morning…*'

It was a good show but not good enough. To be successful the narrative needed to stand on its own two feet, drawing the audience in to a genuine story, but I didn't quite achieve that, meaning that the performance only really worked for those audiences who knew their Dickens and could have fun trying to spot the links, or guessing which passage I was going to use from each novel.

Great Expectations, however, has become one of the shows that I perform often on tour. Great Expectations is my favourite novel, so when I took the decision to adapt it for the stage, I was conscious that I had to honour the original work. Being one of the later novels it is slightly more difficult to adapt, as the plotlines are tightly interwoven throughout the book. In the early novels, such as Nicholas Nickleby, the story tended to involve a character being wrapped up in individual scenes surrounded by amazing characters, before moving on to another setting and a different cast, meaning that it is easy to lift a specific plotline to follow.

My script relies on the ever-present influence of Miss Havisham on Pip and I decided to have her permanently on the stage, overseeing everything. This I achieved by draping a hat stand with white fabric until it took on the appearance of a stately woman with a veil and train. She remains at the rear of the stage until her fiery demise, at which point the fabric lays discarded on the floor.

The tone of the show is much more serious than many

116

others, it is intense and dark with the only comic relief coming from Mr Wemmick and his aged parent. I was worried that my regular audiences would not take to this different style, but it has proved to be a great success with both promoters and public.

In 2006 I was booked to perform on a cruise ship and it was a curious set of circumstances that led to it. P&O Cruises had decided to offer a literary themed trip and had contracted various lecturers to speak on different authors. The booking department had found people who specialised in William Shakespeare, Jane Austen and, I believe, Chaucer, but they were anxious to find a Dickens performer to complete the set, and approached the Charles Dickens Museum for ideas who fortunately suggested me.

I was due to fly to Barcelona where I would join the cruise ship Artemis, the smallest in the P&O fleet and which was dedicated to a more mature clientele, with no children on board. I was to take over from the performer who had been giving a presentation based on the works of Jane Austen, and this was fortunate because the gentleman in question was Anton Rodgers, a well-regarded and renowned actor who had not only enjoyed a long career on stage but had also been extremely popular on TV and film. Thanks to his reputation Anton had been offered a very good contract by P&O, with various privileges not offered to other entertainers working under a crew status. Mr Rodgers had a good passenger cabin and dined in the main restaurants, rather than the officer's mess. He was able to leave the ship as soon as she docked rather than waiting for the crew to be given permission to disembark.

Why am I taking so much time describing the details of another actor's contract? Well, the agent who had booked me also represented Anton and so I was signed to the same deal, meaning that I had a wonderful experience during my years on the ships.

Incidentally there is a connection between Anton Rodgers and *A Christmas Carol* for it is he, playing an undertaker, that sang 'Thank You Very Much!' in the Albert Finney musical film version of the book.

One particular challenge for me was that P&O insisted that all of the shows, or lectures, had to last for forty minutes, not more, not less, so I had to adapt my current shows as well as creating new ones to that duration. Mr Dickens is Coming worked well, as did A Child's Journey with Dickens. Nicholas Nickleby could be shoehorned into the correct timeslot and with a bit of preamble so could Sikes and Nancy.

The theatres on board the ships, especially the larger ones, were amazing spaces with technical equipment that most land-based venues could only dream of. They were mainly used for the large cabaret-style shows in the evenings, either troupes of dancers, or popular comedians and singers. Occasionally, however, they were used during the day for lectures, and this particularly suited my theatrical style.

Although the physical act of performing on a ship was the same as in any other venue, the connection with the audience was completely different in that I was living with them for the duration of the cruise. In a theatre I perform the show, the audience claps (hopefully), I leave the stage, they go home and that may be the last we see of each other, but on a ship the audience is there at breakfast, around the swimming pool, walking the deck and will want to talk. If a show has gone well then there is no better place to be than on a cruise ship, if things have gone badly then there is nowhere to hide.

Word of mouth on board is a powerful tool and on one

cruise across the Atlantic I learned a valuable lesson about the importance of performing well in such an environment. The crossing was to take five days and a full programme of lectures and events had been scheduled, of which I was a part. Another lecturer was a gentleman giving a series of talks on American history with specific reference to the cities we were due to visit. He would talk about the Civil and Revolutionary wars and to me at least, the programme sounded fascinating, and I made a mental note to be at all of his events. Also on the schedule was an ex-police officer from Birmingham who was going to talk about interview techniques in a custody suite, which frankly didn't promise much.

The first lecture on American history was packed, and it was a large theatre, perhaps larger than the gentleman was used to. He stood at the very edge of the huge stage barely visible, illuminated only by the light of his lectern. His talk was supported by a PowerPoint slide show, but some slides were in the wrong position, or didn't appear when he wanted them to. His delivery was quiet and, on occasion, inaudible and soon there was shuffling in the audience as a few people left. His next lecture was less well attended, and the one after that attracted an even smaller following until by the time he spoke for the last time there was only a handful of people in the cavernous space. The frustrating thing about the whole situation was that what he had to say was, indeed, fascinating and well researched, but the talks had no theatricality about them and failed to engage a group of people who wanted entertainment rather than education.

The ex-police officer, on the other hand, worked the ship superbly. Naturally enough his first talk didn't attract a large crowd, but those that were there laughed and clapped and had an amazing time. He spoke without notes, and owned the stage, commanding attention. He told anecdotes and broke away from whatever his daily theme was, which endeared him to his listeners. And after he had finished, people went to the restaurant and the buffet and the bars and told anyone who would listen about what an entertaining time they had had, and how everyone should go to the next talk. Sure enough the theatre was soon full and by the time he gave his last lecture it was a case of standing room only.

The style of the presentation was everything, as well as using the built in PR machine that is a group of people gathered on a ship. Some performers didn't like mingling with passengers, whereas I loved to chat with people over a coffee, go on tours and share dinner tables, meaning that I could get a sense of what they enjoyed and hopefully build the core of a friendly audience who would encourage others to come to my shows too.

During my years of cruising, I visited some amazing countries and saw some incredible sights. I went to the North Cape of Norway in June and spent four days - and nights - in bright sunlight; I woke in my cabin with a view of Sidney Opera House and the bridge; I saw penguins on the Falkland Islands and walked on the Great Wall of China; I was even able to stroll around the Monaco Grand Prix track, thus satisfying an ambition from childhood when I first watched blurry television coverage of the great race and wanted to visit.

I had another reason to be grateful to P&O Cruises too, for it was on Artemis that I first met a pianist named Elizabeth Hayes who had been booked to perform a series of classical recitals on board. Liz and I have been together ever since, and I couldn't do what I do without her love, energy and support.

On dry land many of my British venues were repeat bookings and as I exhausted my repertoire it became obvious that I needed to find some new material. In the back of my mind there was that suggestion from my father about Doctor Marigold and at last I thought I may give it a try. As ever, he had been right with his advice, for I loved it and the audiences loved it. Sadly, he never saw me perform it.

In 2005 I was selected to be the President of the International Dickens Fellowship, and Dad was so proud (he had also held the post in the past and considered it a huge honour). I was to be inaugurated at the annual conference which that year was held in Canterbury, and Dad had asked me to pass on his warmest wishes to his many friends who would be present. On the evening of Saturday 1 August I stood to speak at the grand banquet and spent a long time talking about my father, passing on his greetings and sharing his disappointment that he couldn't be there. I felt a surge of love and warmth for him in the applause that followed. At the conclusion of the dinner, as I walked into the warm summer night, I checked my phone and received the news that even as I had been speaking my father had suffered a heart attack and died in his bed.

I drove straight home to be with my mother that night and had nothing with me but the dinner jacket and flamboyant waistcoat that I had worn at the dinner. I had planned to visit my parents the next day anyway, to tell Dad all about the event, and to prune a rather out of control wisteria that was taking over the front of their house. I felt duty bound to do as I had promised, so on the next morning my parents' neighbours had the strange sight of a man in evening dress precariously balanced atop a ladder hacking away at the woody branches, I am sure that Dad would have laughed until there were tears in his eyes.

My father was the greatest influence in my career, always there with advice and support and a pocket full of loose change! Today, whenever I perform Doctor Marigold I think of him.

With my greatest inspiration – Dad
Photo Credit: Jeneene Brengelman

Chapter 7
Memorable Venues

During my many years of travelling I have been fortunate to have been given the opportunity to perform in some amazing venues, and often these have seen me follow in the footsteps of Charles Dickens.

I have given performances in his two surviving homes, 48 Doughty Street, where The Charles Dickens Museum is based in the Bloomsbury area of London, and at Gad's Hill Place in Kent, the house that as a child he would admire with his father, who told him that if he were to work very hard he may sometime come to own. Gad's Hill Place became a beacon of hope to the young Charles, who overcame all kinds of adversity to eventually purchase it and it was within those walls that he died in 1870.

But the venues that really make an impression on me are the theatres in which Dickens performed when he toured. To stand upon the same boards, to look at the same auditorium, is an extraordinary thing and fills me with a thrill of excitement every time I am lucky enough to walk into the lights.

St George's Hall, Liverpool

In England the venue that I am most familiar with is The Concert Room at the St George's Hall, in Liverpool, where I perform to sell-out crowds each Christmas season. Charles visited Liverpool on many occasions, and in 1843 it was where he departed from to sail to America for the first time. Dickens always loved port towns (he had been born in Portsmouth and grew up in and around the Royal Naval dockyard at Chatham), for he felt a restlessness, an urgency, a sense of adventure to them.

On one occasion in Liverpool Dickens spent a night with the local constabulary, having become a temporary special constable, and saw the true grit and underbelly of the city at first hand. He used the experiences of that night to write chapters of 'The Uncommercial Traveller'.

When he began his reading tours in 1858 it was inevitable that he would include Liverpool in his schedule, and he first performed in The Philharmonic Hall which had a capacity of 2,300. His shows were all sold out.

In January 1862 Charles returned to Liverpool to read again (in fact he had been in the city to give readings on 15 December 1861, but had cancelled his appearance due to the sudden death of Prince Albert). On this occasion he forsook the Philharmonic Hall and appeared instead in The Concert Room at St George's Hall, a much smaller venue, seating around five hundred. He adored the intimacy that the space offered and dubbed it as 'the most perfect hall in the world'. A few years ago I was invited to perform at St George's Hall and as soon as I stood on the stage and started to rehearse I understood his appreciation for the space. The stage is high, and dominates the room, giving a performer a real sense of power. The floor level seating extends back a little way and then a few low steps create two or three rows of tired seating beneath the balcony, which extends all of the way to the stage in a great semi-circle. The pillars on the stage are gilded with gold, and the room is lighted with a giant chandelier, whose tiny crystal droplets gently chime as the heat rises from the floor, making them quiver against one another. It is strange, but it is that chiming that gives me a feeling of connection to Charles Dickens in The Concert Room. I don't know if that particular chandelier hung in Dickens's day, but I like to think that the little tinkling sound would be as familiar to him as it is to me.

The audiences in Liverpool are vocal and energetic, and the sound of them all clapping, cheering and stamping their feet on the old wooden floorboards at the conclusion of the show is one of the most exciting sounds I know.

The Tremont Theatre, Boston

In 1867 Charles Dickens travelled to the United States to perform his readings in cities on the Eastern seaboard. His base was in Boston, where he stayed at The Parker House Hotel, right next door to the Tremont Theatre, where he gave his performances, and in 1999 I was booked to perform in the same theatre and to stay in the same hotel. By the time I first visited the hall, the Tremont had been converted into a Baptist Chapel, but the space is the one that Dickens would have seen when he first visited in November 1867 and wrote that 'The hall is charming – I never saw a better!' and when he and his tour manager George Dolby tested the room's acoustics, they pronounced it perfect. The readings in Boston were a huge financial and critical success, each event selling out and being the talk of the town.

In 1999 a small group of professional theatre folk, comprising two producers, a stage manager and a publicist, joined forces to promote a show for me in the Tremont Temple, as it is now called.

I first saw the theatre on 6 November of that year and recorded in my diary that 'It hasn't changed a great deal and suddenly the enormity of what I'm doing hits me. I have a very large attack of nerves. It's fascinating and terrifying in equal parts to sit in the auditorium and wonder what Charles Dickens looked like on that stage. How did he sound? How much did he move? The house, of course, would have been filled to capacity, what was the noise of the audience like? All rather scary!'

The performance was on 27 November, and when I arrived at the theatre I was once again overwhelmed by the sheer scale of the situation: 'Everywhere I look there are people doing their jobs. Here is the lighting crew plotting lights, there is the sound man testing his equipment, over there are the front of house crew acquainting themselves with their particular areas. Everywhere is a bustle, everyone getting ready for the performance – my performance. All of a sudden it hits me; all these people are here for me!'

When the audience began to arrive, I found a little alcove just outside my dressing room from where I could watch the auditorium fill up and this is something I like to do if it is possible, for being a solitary actor in a dressing room can be a very lonely thing. By watching a gathering audience, or even just listening to them from behind a curtain, it gives me a feeling of connection with the people I am about to share the next ninety minutes of my life with. On that November afternoon in 1999 I listened to the crowd and wrote that 'It is nearly a full house and there is a very expectant chat. My heart is beating faster and harder.' The show was delayed for fifteen minutes because of the weight of traffic in the area and the difficulty of getting such a large crowd seated, therefore prolonging my fear, and heightening my nerves, but as soon as I took to the stage and started to speak, my mind became clear, and I relished every second of the show.

'The audience are hanging on every word and gesture, and I am leading them here and there.' I wrote. 'At the end the applause is very loud, and I come back for three calls, the theatre standing. It strikes me that I came into Charles Dickens' theatre this morning. Now, it is mine!' OK, that last line was terribly arrogant, but when a show goes well and ticks all of the right boxes, there really is a very intense feeling of ownership, the adrenaline is surging, and you feel as if you could do anything. I certainly felt it that night at The Tremont.

I returned to Boston and The Tremont Temple the following year and once again the atmosphere and the occasion were wonderful, but nothing could ever match the sheer excitement of that first performance.

The Mechanics Hall, Worcester, Massachusetts

Charles Dickens' American reading tour was built around long runs in Boston and New York, but it also included one-night stands in venues along the way, one of which was in Worcester Massachusetts, less than fifty miles from Boston. The Mechanics Hall had been built just ten years before and was the only venue in the city capable of holding an event such as a Dickens reading.

The day booked for the performance was 23 March, a Monday, and many of the tickets were sold to the large farming community which dominated the region. There was due to be a poultry sale in town on the day after Dickens' performance, so rather than making an extra round trip many of the farmers brought their stock with them and made arrangements to stay in the city overnight. When it was realised that there would be a large amount of caged fowl present, the owners of The Mechanics Hall offered a room where they could all be kept.

The grand building was designed in the Italianate style

and seated nearly two thousand people. The various spaces range over three floors: at street level there is a lobby and from there two staircases, one to each side, take the audience to the first floor where there is a fairly plain hall (The Washburn Hall which is where the poultry were being held) and then up again to the particularly grand auditorium which is of course where Dickens would be reading his two most popular pieces: A Christmas Carol and The Trial from The Pickwick Papers.

The audience were requested to take their seats ten minutes before the commencement of the performance, and so they waited in eager anticipation. With five minutes to go a figure walked onto the stage, was this Charles Dickens? Surely not, but who? This was actually Dickens' gas man who had responsibility for the lighting system that travelled with Charles. The lighting rig framed the performer with two upright pipes with reflecting lights fixed at head height, and then an overhead bar with more lights shining down upon the reader. Before Dickens took the stage the gasman would open the valves to let the gas flow, and so the lights would begin to brighten until they threw, as Mark Twain noted, 'a glory upon the scene'. Unfortunately, the light was so bright that it shone through the cracks in the floorboards thereby illuminating the Washburn Hall below and waking the cockerels who quite naturally started to crow loudly, assuming that morning had broken. The first hour of Dickens' performance was accompanied by this cacophony.

In 2012, I was booked to recreate Charles' reading at The Mechanics Hall, and as in Boston I had been called upon to give many interviews before the event, which guaranteed a good turnout. On the evening of 21 September the crowds gathered outside the Mechanic's Hall, as they had done 144 years before, albeit without the livestock, and made their way up the twin staircases and into The Great Hall on the top floor. The show was being produced by my great friends The Vaillancourt family, and they went out their way to make the entire experience as memorable to me as they could.

At seven-thirty Gary Vaillancourt stood on the stage to welcome the audience and to introduce me and when he finished his remarks, he left the stage and I proudly strode on to it, in the footsteps of my great-great-grandfather. But the Vaillancourts had a trick up their sleeve, for as I stepped into the light, the hall resounded to a recording of cockerels loudly crowing thus drowning out my introductory remarks!

Edgar Allen Poe's Graveside, Baltimore.

In the very early years of my touring days, in 1997, Caroline arranged for me to meet David Keltz an actor who portrayed Edgar Allen Poe, and had done so to great critical acclaim for many years. Before we met, Caroline took me to watch one of David's performances in the prestigious National Press Club in the heart of Washington DC. To be honest, I was rather in awe of him, for he seemed to embrace everything that 'being an actor' was. I have always had a slight inferiority complex because I didn't formally study theatre, so when I come face to face with a performer who has studied technique and preparation, I get quite defensive. David's performance was intense, considered, brilliant and oh, so professional. As I watched, I thought of my show – a collection of silly voices and little more and felt even more insecure about myself.

Caroline's idea had been to bring two great authors together and David had suggested performing a little improvised scene at Poe's graveside during the evening of Halloween. One of the pieces that David performed as Poe was *'The Tell-Tale Heart'* in which the story's narrator attempts to convince the reader that he is not insane, by describing a 'perfect' murder that he has committed, before being tormented by a knocking apparently from beneath the floorboards where he has hidden the body. The officers who are questioning him about the old man's disappearance, do not hear the knocking but the narrator confesses anyway and pleads that the boards be lifted so that his crime is exposed.

David suggested to me that it would be fun if Dickens and Poe had a discussion about the remarkable similarities between Poe's classic piece and 'A Confession Found in a Prison Cell from the Time of Charles II' by Charles Dickens. My low opinion of myself fell even further, for I had never even heard of this piece! I now know it appeared as a short story in Master Humphrey's Clock, and was originally published in 1840, two years before *The Tell-Tale Heart*, and that very few people have ever heard of it.

The idea was that David should just be about to begin *The Tell-Tale Heart* when the figure of Dickens would emerge from the shadows of the graveyard and begin to berate Poe that the story is nothing but cheap plagiarism. Caroline suggested that the two of us disappear into the crypt of the nearby chapel and work out what we were going to do. And it was then that our different worlds and backgrounds united, for we began to improvise our little scene and it was exciting, and we bonded.

When the audience gathered later that night, in the cold and dark, I loitered in the deep shadows while David began his performance until it was time do my piece. I strode through the audience with all of the energy that Dickens possessed waving my cane in the air, and shouted down this dapper, moustachioed figure. Poe in turn defended his work as a classic, pointing out that the Dickens piece was nothing more than a 'pot boiler'. Our short scene played to its conclusion with me ceding to Poe's protestations and letting him recite his work.

That evening marked the beginning of a long friendship with David and we still meet every year as he and his wife Teresa make a point of coming to one of my shows when I am touring. We meet for dinner afterwards and we chat and we laugh and we tell theatrical anecdotes long into the night.

A few years later, David mentioned to me that an audience member came up to him after one of his shows and said, "I don't know if you remember, but I was at a performance you did at the graveside, when this stranger just interrupted your show and started complaining about some Dickens thing – it was weird!"

David is still intense and precise, whilst I am still loud and flamboyant, and the wonderful thing is, that is OK – we both suit 'our' authors, and we both bring joy and happiness to our audiences.

Highclere Castle

A venue that has only recently become part of my tour is the grand old ancestral home of the Caernarvon family, Highclere Castle. Highclere is, of course, more famously known as the setting for the long running television series 'Downton Abbey', and to approach the old castle along the winding driveway is to be part of a familiar scene, and as I swish through the gravel to stop at the great front door, I always fully expect the liveried staff to be there, greeting me.

In fact, Lord and Lady Caernarvon still own and live in the house and open it to visitors during the Summer months. Of course, the television – and now film - connection brings in many visitors, but the family has a remarkable story to tell in its own right: The fifth Earl was responsible for funding Howard Carter's archaeological dig which uncovered the treasures of the Pharaoh Tutankhamun, whilst the seventh Earl became one of the leading racehorse trainers in England at the nearby Highclere Stud, and in that capacity enjoyed a long and close relationship with Queen Elizabeth II as her racing manager.

My performance space at Highclere is in the great central hallway, or saloon as it is called. A small stage is set up in front of the fireplace and to my left a huge Christmas tree towers up to the second-floor gallery and beyond, flamboyantly decorated. The audience is small in number, maybe eighty or so, and are gathered around me on three sides, making for a wonderfully intimate experience.

When I first saw the space, I decided that I would make my first entrance down the great wooden staircase, through the audience and up onto the stage. This purpose was less to do with any sense of theatricality (nobody in the audience would actually see my descent, as the stairs are behind them) but more because that was the staircase on the telly! It is a very strange sensation to perform in a space that is so very familiar to me, and I have to concentrate even harder than usual, for I am surrounded by the 'ghosts' of Downton – that was the corner where Matthew first embraced Lady Mary as his fiancé Lavinia looked on from that balcony. Here is the very spot where Dame Nelly Melba sang to the family and staff, and there is the bedroom in which Mr Pamuk slept – and died. With all that whirring around my head, it is sometimes difficult to bring my mind back to the events of Christmas Eve 1843.

Highclere is a happy to place to perform, the family and staff being cheerful and generous hosts indeed. The house could have been built to celebrate Christmas and I always feel a very special excitement as I sit alone in the saloon before the show, taking in the splendour of my surroundings and remembering how lucky I am to be able to do what I do.

Buckingham Palace, London

This one is a slightly cheeky one to include, for I have never performed at Buckingham Palace and neither did Charles Dickens, but we did both meet the Monarch of our respective days within the walls of that fine old house.

Being one of the most revered and eminent Victorians it is of little surprise that opportunities for Dickens to meet the Queen were neither few nor far between, but it took a long time for it to actually happen.

The first chance had come in 1857, when Charles Dickens had formed an amateur theatrical company to perform a series of plays to raise money in support of the families of impoverished artists and actors, called The Guild of Literature and Art. The plays had created quite a stir in London and Dickens had converted his own house into a theatre to stage a production of a piece called The Frozen Deep, written by his good friend Wilkie Collins. Such had been the popularity of the event that Dickens was keen to repeat it and his opportunity came when fellow writer Douglas Jerrold suddenly died. Charles immediately announced that The Frozen Deep would be reprised to raise money for the Jerrold family. Because the event was to be a charity one, Dickens had written to Buckingham Palace to ask the Queen for her patronage. A reply came back that Victoria could not bless the performance with her support, for it would set a precedent, but she did particularly want to see the play, and therefore invited the entire company to Buckingham Palace for a private showing.

Dickens refused the invitation, the official reason he gave

was that his daughters were in the cast, and he didn't want them to appear at Court in the guise of 'actresses' with all of the low connotations that the profession held at that time. I think that he had also spent so much time and effort having the set and scenery built for the public show that the idea of taking it all down to be moved to the Palace and then transported back again, just for a single performance, appalled his sense of theatre. The performance would not be at Buckingham Palace; however, Queen Victoria was invited to a private viewing at The Gallery of Illustration in Regent Street on the day before the fundraiser. His daughters and sister-in-law remained in the cast.

The play was a great success and after watching a short farce, which finished off the evening's events, the Queen sent a note inviting Dickens to come into the auditorium so that she could thank him personally (in a letter to a friend Dickens suggested that Victoria was 'begging' to see him). However, Charles was still in the costume from the farce and refused to meet his Monarch.

Years later, when he was on his reading tours, Victoria again wrote to him, inviting him to the Palace to read for her there. One more Charles declined the opportunity, rather arrogantly writing that 'I do not perform for individuals!'

Eventually, however, in the last months of his life Charles accepted an invitation from the Queen to meet her at a private audience, and the two spent some thirty minutes together in Buckingham Palace, talking about his novels, and about his recent trip to the United States. Dickens, although in agony from gout, stood respectfully throughout the meeting. He showed Victoria some photographs taken during the American Civil War and they discussed his forthcoming book, *The Mystery of Edwin Drood*, he even offered to tell her how the story was going to end, but she declined, suggesting that she wished to read the unfolding plot as it was published. Of course, Dickens was not able to finish Drood and his death, at the age of only fifty-eight, three months after his conversation with Victoria, left us with a mystery that has never been solved.

In 2012 the nation celebrated the 200th anniversary of Charles Dickens' birth and the most prestigious event was a reception at Buckingham Palace hosted by Queen Elizabeth II and The Duke of Edinburgh. Invitations were received by famous actors who have performed in adaptations of the novels, academics who have studied and written about Charles' life, and members of the family: Liz and I were truly fortunate to have been included on the list.

On 14 February we drove our car through the great gates in front of the palace and parked in the courtyard before walking under the famous portico, up the small flight of steps and into the Queen's official London residence.

We ascended the grand staircase and made our way into a gilded and packed reception room, in which there seemed to be celebrities at every corner. We were given a glass of champagne and waiters circulated with plates of hors d'oeuvre, beautifully created to allow for single-bite ease of eating. Somehow, seamlessly, we discovered ourselves in a long line and at the head of it we were presented to the Queen and the Duke, who shook our hands and said a few words, before moving on to the next guests. If that wasn't enough of a thrill, the members of the family were gathered up and taken to a smaller room, where we were granted a second and more private audience with the Queen, who spent ten minutes or so chatting with us all, demonstrating a remarkable memory as she recalled meeting my Uncle Peter many years previously, wistfully remembering that he had been 'rather dishy'. Peter had been a Royal Naval officer on Motor Torpedo Boats during world two.

Queen Elizabeth was quite amazing, the energy she demonstrated as she worked the room, making intelligent conversation with all of these literary and artistic folks, was remarkable. And the next evening, or later in the week, she would be talking to nuclear physicists, or footballers, or politicians, and she would share the same beaming smile with them and display the same levels of knowledge of their work and would delight them as she had delighted us.

Nobody quite knows how we knew when to leave, but suddenly there was a gentle flow of people towards the door and the staircase, so we all dutifully followed: nobody actually told us that it was time to go, it just happened.

Downstairs in the hall, as we prepared to leave, Liz said that she needed to freshen up, so I waited for her, standing close to the main door. As I stood, a friend put on his coat and made for the exit, and we briefly exchanged pleasantries before I said 'goodbye' to him, and he walked into the February evening. Coincidentally, another friend was next in line, and I wished him goodnight also. An actor who I had admired in a Dickens adaptation then came down the steps and we had a brief chat before I held the door open to let him out. As he walked away calling out 'goodnight' the realisation came to me that it was if I were bidding farewell to my own guests, as if I owned the Palace – it was tempting to shout after them 'could you lock the gate as you leave?' When Liz re-joined me my moment of fantasy grandeur came to an end, and we too walked across the courtyard and back into our normal life.

Chapter 8
Return to America

Following my retirement from a life on the roads of America I made sure that I had plenty of bookings to perform in England, but when November turned into December I just did not have that buzz, that sense of excitement, that adrenaline rush which had accompanied me for over ten years. But, I told myself, I had enjoyed an amazing time and had seen some incredible sights, but I needed to accept and honour the decision that I had made – a chapter of my life had closed for good.

Until an email arrived from Mr Bob Byers Junior.

Back in 2002 Caroline had told me that there would be a special guest coming to one of my shows at The Hotel Hershey to evaluate my performance and see if the company in question might want to book me for the following season. The company, Caroline told me, was an all-American success story, a small business that had been started on a kitchen table and had now grown into one of the largest manufacturers of Christmas collectibles in the country.

In the 1970s a young fashion designer called Joyce Byers had decided to make some Christmas table-centre ornaments, rather than spending what little precious money she had on expensive shop-bought ones. At the table Joyce began to fashion a rudimentary skeleton shape from an old wire coat hanger, which she 'fleshed out' with tissue paper. The face was made with modelling clay and its mouth was formed into a little 'o' shape, as if it were in the middle of signing a

Christmas carol, and so the first Caroller was made. He was joined by a few others and took pride of place on the Byers' Christmas table and the little group were admired by friends who came to visit, so that, before she knew it, Joyce had requests to make more of the figurines and soon they were being taken by local stores. It became apparent that there was a huge demand across the country for genuine American-made goods, and in 1978 Byers' Choice Ltd was formed. Joyce's husband, Bob Snr, had enjoyed a successful career in construction, now turned his considerable business and marketing skills to the new family firm. Byers' Choice grew and grew and soon the couple's sons, Bob Jnr and Jeff, joined the firm which was now based in a huge manufacturing facility, complete with a large visitor centre and store, in Chalfont Pennsylvania.

The fact that the figurines produced at Byers' Choice are called Carollers means that the company celebrates Christmas well and my performance fitted into their marketing plan perfectly. At The Hotel Hershey in 2002 Bob Jnr had been due to come on a fact-finding mission and to talk with Caroline and me about the possibility of the visitor centre becoming a venue for my performance. Sadly for Bob he put his back out and at the last moment he delegated a trusted member of his staff to take the trip in his stead, meaning that I met Lisa Porter, who would become a central part of my touring life, for the first time.

Lisa obviously took a good report back to Chalfont for in 2003 I was booked to perform for Byers' Choice and it was quite an experience. Bob and the family, by which I mean the entire staff, completely cleared the main manufacturing floor in the factory to create an eight hundred-seat theatre. Against one wall a large high stage was installed, whilst theatrical lighting and a sound system was brought in for the shows. I still perform in the same space and Bob jokes that he feels like Mr Fezziwig on Christmas eve, clearing away the warehouse for the great party.

I adored performing at Byers' Choice, although the shows were completely exhausting, and then of course came the signing sessions. For Caroline the sales aspect of my shows was vital and, as I have already mentioned, her contracts with venues were very strict and stipulated that I would only sign products purchased from her stock. At Byers' Choice I was signing in their store and the majority of the audience were collectors of the Carollers, but contractually I was not allowed to sign them. This led to all sorts of unpleasantness and shenanigans behind the scenes and the relationship between Caroline Jackson and Byers' Choice never really recovered from that time on, even though I continued to perform there each year, until my contract with Caroline came to an end and I announced my retirement.

As I have mentioned I found 'retirement' a struggle and after a second season without touring I was becoming frustrated at home until early in 2008 Bob Byers emailed me once again to invite me to attend the Byers' Choice 30th anniversary celebrations, which were due to be held in the September of that year. The thought of returning to Chalfont was appealing but knowing how much effort and expense went into securing a visa it seemed to be a vain hope. I replied to Bob with the sad news that it would a logistical nightmare to secure the correct permission just for a single weekend, and I must regretfully decline the invitation. I do not know for certain, but I think that Bob may be a very good game fisherman, for having gently lured me with bait, he struck quickly and suggested that a possible solution would be to apply for a visa not only for the birthday celebrations but also a subsequent tour as well… only if I were interested, of course. I leapt at the idea.

And so, in 2009 a new Christmas tour arose from the ashes of the old.

In certain ways the new tour was no different to the old one, in that the show was unchanged, and the wide variety of venues presented the same challenges and opportunities as before, indeed many of the old venues came back on board – Mid-Continent Public Library, Hotel Hershey, Williamsburg Inn, The Golden Goose in Occoquan and of course Byers' Choice all featured, but in many other ways the tour was completely different. Firstly, I didn't have anyone travelling with me, whereas Caroline would mostly come to the venues with me, either driving me there or flying with me and managing the events.

Although most venues did offer some merchandise for sale after my shows, there was not the high-pressure sales sessions of the Jackson Enterprise years, when often the signing was longer than the show itself.

Many of the new venues were businesses who worked with Byers' Choice, some were Christmas stores who stocked the Carollers and others were also manufacturers – not business rivals, but companies bringing the same ideal of Christmas to the American market.

The schedule for my tour was much more carefully planned so that, rather than rushing for early morning flights almost every day I would spend much more time in a single region and have the luxury of driving between venues. I love to drive and find it a relaxing way to spend a few hours, and it means that you are much less beholden to weather and technology, and you can be fairly confident that your bags are at least in the same vehicle, heading to the same destination.

Bob asked Lisa Porter, who had originally come to Hershey, to manage my tours and, alongside her regular work at Byers' Choice, she liaised with every venue and made sure that all of the details for my performances were in place – the correct furniture for my show would be there, a good sound system if I needed it, hotels, transport, food etc. Lisa left nothing to chance.

Having learned my own lessons, I worked with Bob and Lisa to ensure that I would only perform a maximum twice a day, and that we built rest days into the schedule, and allowed whole days for long travelling. The result was that I could remain in a single region (New England, for instance, or the Mid-West), and could drive from venue to venue giving me plenty of time to see the world go by and to really enjoy my surroundings, and it was in these years that I began to write my blog.

Initially the blog served three purposes, primarily it was to keep my family in England fully up to date with what I was doing and how the tour was progressing. Secondly my daily report was a way of keeping in touch with Lisa and the team at Byers' Choice, so that they could get a sense of the trip and see where changes or improvements could be made in future years (we always have a de-brief at the tour's end, but there is nothing like the emotion of the moment to paint a true picture). Finally, the blog gave my audiences along the way a sense of inclusion, to make them feel part of my tour. Often people will ask about various things that I have written about – whether a slight cold had improved, whether a costume malfunction had been successfully repaired. Occasionally I might have mentioned that I missed a certain brand of biscuits, and sure enough someone would hand me a gift-wrapped parcel containing the product. One year I jokingly suggested that I would like a Ferrari to drive on my tour and a few weeks later a gentleman gave me a small toy version, apologising that it was not a real one.

Lisa was always on the end of the phone, so if anything

went awry, she was able to sort the problem out instantly: delayed flights, revised travel plans, changes of schedule, but most of all retrieving things that I had left along the way. Watches, fountain pens, pieces of costume and cufflinks have all been left in various dressing rooms and Lisa patiently contacted whoever had booked me and arranged for the items to be sent back to Byers' Choice, or onward to meet up with me at another venue.

The new era of touring meant that I started to forge new friendships in new cities and many of those became permanent fixtures on my schedule:

Vaillancourt Folk Art, Sutton Massachusetts

The Vaillancourts, Judi and Gary, run a company which in many ways is similar to Byers' Choice, in that they produce hand-made Christmas ornaments. While Joyce Byers had a background in fashion and fabric, Judi Vaillancourt is a trained artist and developed a fascination in collecting antique chocolate moulds and began to experiment by using them to create plaster Santa Claus figures, which she would then carefully paint and decorate. In the same way that Bob Byers Snr used his business background to support Joyce, so Gary did the same and soon Vaillancourt Folk Art was created. Staff were taken on to make the figures and others to paint them, initially from the family home, but eventually the business found a home in a beautiful old Victorian mill building, which is not only a manufacturing facility, but also the most magical store you have ever seen. Judi and Gary are still very hands on and have been joined in recent years by their son Luke who brings a contemporary flair to the marketing of a most traditional craft.

The Byers and the Vaillancourt families have always been close, so it was natural for Bob to offer my show to Judi and Gary when I began touring again in 2009, and they leapt at the chance. Within the old mill building is a room that was unused, and it was here that a theatre, called The Blaxton Hall, was created each Thanksgiving weekend. Being quite a small room, the audience are packed up close to the stage on three sides, creating a very intimate atmosphere, with lots of opportunity for ad-libbed repartee. The stage is spacious, giving me plenty of room to roam and it is beautifully designed and painted by Judi, so it is as if I am in Scrooge's own rooms. Stage lighting and a good sound system complete the package and the tour would now feel incomplete without my visit to Sutton.

Mind you, it has not always been plain sailing, and one year I very nearly didn't make the show at all. I had been due to fly to Boston and then drive in a rental car to Sutton, but thick fog prevented my plane from leaving and the many hours of spare time that I had soon passed. I sat helpless in a terminal building whilst phone calls dashed hither and thither between Lisa, the Vaillancourts and myself. Eventually, we found another flight which would get me to Boston, albeit late, and it was arranged that Luke would be waiting to pick me up at the kerbside and rush me to the theatre. As I sat on my plane, the audience were gathering and there was no show for them to see. It was Luke's father-in-law Bob who saved the day, he grasped his trusty guitar and stepped on to the stage and took on the responsibility of entertaining the crowd. I seem to remember that he only had three songs: The Streets of London, Greensleeves and one other that I can't remember now, and he played them as if on a repeating loop, but the audience at Vaillancourt Folk Art are a kind and generous bunch and by the time I rushed into the room there was such a great atmosphere that the show couldn't fail to be a success. It was a tight call, and when in the show I awoke as Scrooge, on Christmas morning and threw the curtains open to see that there was 'no fog', everyone cheered loudly.

My shows in Sutton are always over the Thanksgiving weekend and the Vaillancourt family have often been kind enough to invite me to celebrate this most American holiday in their company. They have become good and close friends and I always enjoy my time with them.

The Inn at Christmas Place, Pigeon Forge, Tennessee

Another new venue that came onboard thanks to Byers' Choice was a little hotel in the tourist town of Pigeon Forge at the foot of the Smoky Mountains in Tennessee. I knew nothing about Pigeon Forge and had no idea what to expect when I first visited. I flew into Knoxville airport, picked up a rental car, set my satellite navigation unit and followed the directions. My route took me to the town of Sevierville, and then onto route 241 towards my destination, and a series of extraordinary sights were awaiting me – there was the huge prow of the Titanic towering above me, and next to it a typical antebellum southern mansion which was upside down, to the left-hand side I saw King Kong clinging onto the top of the Empire State Building, it all seemed most odd. Years before when I had first visited Myrtle Beach I had described it in my diary as being like 'Las Vegas, without the good taste', and the same thought came to me now, for every building was pretending to be something else. As I made my way up this southern version of The Strip I began to doubt if a show based on a classic work by a British author had any future in this environment. How wrong could I have been? On arriving at The Inn, a hotel across the street from the Incredible Christmas Place store I was given the most genuine and generous of welcomes. The Inn does not cater for the one-night business clientele, but is a home for those enjoying everything that Pigeon Forge and nearby Gatlinburg have to offer. The guests are in town to have fun and relax. My performances were staged in a small dining room in the basement, which never required any form of amplification or stage effects. It was a simple and pure way of telling the story.

The joy about The Inn at Christmas Place was that most of the audience were staying at the hotel, so there existed a weekend house party feel to the event. On the morning after a show my 'theatre' would be the breakfast room and as I piled my plate high from the sumptuous buffet, people would come and chat about the show and many became good friends. On one occasion I noticed the most spectacular Corvette bearing the license plate 'Thx Santa' parked outside the hotel and wrote about it in my blog. In no time I received an email from the car's owner Gary, who was a regular attendee at my shows, offering me the opportunity to drive the beautiful machine, and the next time we were both in Pigeon Forge Gary and I drove up into the mountains for an hour or so during which the Victorian era and *A Christmas Carol* was forgotten completely, and I just kept making unnecessary gear changes just so that I could hear the engine burble.

Ready to head into the mountains
Photo Credit: Author's Collection

A few years ago, I shortened my tour to spend more time at home, and Pigeon Forge dropped off my schedule, but I have amazing memories and very much hope that I can return one day.

Douglas County Historical Society, Omaha, Nebraska

In the very centre of America, equidistant from sea to shining sea is the city of Omaha, Nebraska which is home to The Douglas County Historical Society, an organisation that was formed to preserve the archives and tell the history of that area. The Society is based in The General Cook House, a small mansion proudly overlooking the former Fort Omaha, and among the volunteers there is Suzy Phillips, a passionate collector of all things Dickens. Suzy first saw me perform at The Williamsburg Inn and thought that an appearance in Omaha would benefit the Historical Association, so she marched into the office of Kathy Aultz, the society's new director, who had barely got her feet under the desk, and told her that there should be a fact-finding mission to Excelsior Springs in Missouri, where I was to perform at The Elms Hotel.

Kathy was obviously impressed enough to reach out to Byers' Choice and I was engaged to journey to the Mid-West where a performance in Omaha could be linked to my annual visit to the Kansas City region, and I have been performing for DCHS ever since, and I love my time there.

In a 2015 blog post I wrote, 'I am heading to Omaha, and I have noticed over the years that certain cities illicit certain responses from people. For example, when I say I am going to Williamsburg people sigh with pleasure and say 'oh, how beautiful;' when I mention Minneapolis people will mock-shiver and say 'brrrrr. Hope you've packed your long-johns.' When I tell people I am going to Omaha people look at me, almost horror struck, and then say – placing the rising, questioning emphasis on the final syllable OmaHA? Why?'

'It is very unfair; Omaha is a wonderful city with great people in it and I am happy to stand up and fight its corner! I suppose that part of Omaha's problem is that it isn't near anywhere – it is geographically in the centre of the country, so east coast and west coast alike can mock with impunity.'

My performances in Omaha are spread out over a few days, sometimes I will visit a local high school to perform for the students, and on other occasions I have gone to book shops to give ad-libbed talks about the life of Charles Dickens, but the main shows are traditionally spread over two venues. The first is a performance of A Christmas Carol at the Field Club, a golf club in the city. In a grand ballroom a narrow stage is set up with the minimum of props. Some of the performances are after a lavish tea service where the guests sip out of bone China cups before placing them on bone China saucers. When the room is thus set up with linen-covered tables I let my show spread from the stage and involve the audiences as I used to in the hotels, but when the room is laid out with theatre-style seating I confine my activities to the stage itself.

When I introduced sound effects to my show (initially just the opening music), we discovered that the Field Club had an issue – the only way to play music in the room was to use the amplifying system for the entire complex, which was situated far away in a small cupboard off the reception area. To get the cue on time I would stand at the corner of the room, by the door (fortunately I made my first entrance through the audience), and when Kathy had finished her introduction on the stage, I would wave to a member of the Field Club staff, who would in turn wave to a colleague in the cupboard, who would then hit the 'play' button. It was all very awkward, but these days the club has a system in the room itself, which makes things much easier.

I am lucky at The Field Club, for Suzy's husband, Lee, is a member there and looks after me when I am not performing. We will have lunch in a tiny bar known as The Cry Room, where golfers drown their sorrows after a frustrating round on the course, and my changing room is in the locker room, where a Victorian frock coat looks incongruous next to the golfing attire.

The second regular venue in Omaha is at General Crook House itself, where a tiny stage is erected in the window alcove of the dining room. Chairs are packed in to create an audience of, maybe, forty or so, creating a very intimate atmosphere, very suited for a Victorian reading. My smaller performances are the ones that work well in the Crook House, such as Doctor Marigold, The Signalman and Sikes and Nancy, and one can almost imagine Charles Dickens himself regaling a group of friends in his own London house. A sense of tradition and ceremony has built up around my evenings at The Crook House, and after the show is finished the entire audience move into the adjoining room where glasses of champagne await. Suzy will have written a toast, which includes references to all of the shows that I have performed during that year's visit, and the evening ends with the celebratory clinking of glasses.

I have an alter ego in Omaha, for a few years ago a life sized carboard cut out of myself was produced to help publicize my visits, this fellow becoming affectionately known as 'Flat Gerald'.

The Mid Continent Public Library
The visits to Omaha are always linked to my performances for the Mid-Continent Public Library Service in the Kansas City area of Missouri, for the two venues are connected by a single road, I29, which has to be one of the dullest stretches of road

148

in the world, it is straight, flat and featureless. In 2017 I had the misfortune to do the journey twice in less than a week. Having performed in Omaha I drove to Missouri, but having finished my two days there had to drive back to Omaha for another day of performing. I had exhausted all of my descriptive powers about the I29 on my first journey so had nothing left to write in my blog for the second, so I decided to write about the journey in the style of one my favourite authors, Ian Fleming. I had been listening to unabridged audiobooks of the Bond novels that season, and so placed myself in the leading role:

'Cocooned deep within the scarlet Hyundai, Dickens slipped his fingers sensually to the small hidden lever that would set the cruise control, and as the car surged towards the seventy MPH limit he relaxed and his mind wandered back to the events that had brought him to this moment.

Two hours earlier the sky had been inky black as he emerged from the hotel. The night manager had been attentive and confirmed that there were no charges on the account. It was of no consequence to Dickens, he knew that all of the charges had been picked up by his employer.

The experienced spy never relaxes, to do so could mean the failure of a mission, or worse. So even in the early hours, with tiredness still wrapping itself around him, Dickens had naturally noticed that the manager's name was Squire (the badge on his shirt had stolen his anonymity – a mistake that Dickens would never let himself make). Squire had worn a striped shirt of royal blue and white, that may have been handmade in Saville Row. The tie had been a garish mix of blues and pinks, and the combination proved that Squire was not a man driven by convention. Dickens approved of him, and the positive image was confirmed by a firm dry handshake and a conspiratorial smile.

'Drive Safe!' Dickens grunted a reply and wondered what his English master at Fettes School would have made of that dropped final syllable?

The Hyundai (the 2.4 litre, 4-cylinder model with the flattened tail pipe) burbled into life as Dickens flicked his fingers over the device that Q branch had provided for this mission. The 'Tom Tom' unit (jokingly named after Thomas Tom from the Quartermaster's design office, who was responsible for producing this masterpiece) would give him precise directions to anywhere in the United States. Dickens sighed, he missed the days of an old-fashioned map, but knew that his survival relied upon such technology.

The readout informed him that the journey would take two hours and fifty-six minutes, and he sent a silent word of thanks to Tom. Before caressing the transmission to drive, Dickens took a sip of the hot coffee in a paper mug. The drink was rich and strong and immediately the caffeine coursed through his veins. He smiled grimly and reflected that today he would need all of the help he could get. As he drained the last of the liquid he crushed the cup and lusted for his royal blue Minton China service, with the three gold rings around the rim, at home.

The ice was clearing from the windscreen now, and he swung the steering wheel to the left, guiding the beast onto the empty road. The low-profile Pirellis briefly objected, but Dickens was an expert and in no time the rubber gripped the tarmacadam surface and propelled him towards Omaha and his destiny.

In the darkness he caught a brief glimpse of his face reflected in the glass – a face ravaged by so many years of such missions. He grimaced at the memory of the young man who once would have gazed back at him with clear eyes, a cruel mouth and a comma of dark hair falling carelessly over his forehead. What would that young man think if he knew how soon that comma would be deleted, thought Dickens.

For a moment Dickens pulled himself back to the present, the Sonata was eating up the miles, but the road demanded his full attention. He had been driving with that built-in auto pilot that every high-quality driver possesses, but now every fibre of his being was required to execute a dangerous and complicated manoeuvre: the I29 curved gently to the left, Dickens let his left-hand drop, pulling the soft leather of the wheel down, simultaneously pushing his right hand higher.

Would the car respond? Dammit, turn dammit, TURN! On the edge of the road a carcass of an animal lay mutilated. If he couldn't complete this turn he would become its eternal companion.

No! the car was not turning, and beads of sweat began to form, but Dickens lived for moments such as this, it was his reason for being, and all of the training had prepared him for split seconds of such danger. He was resolute, holding the wheel lightly (the less experienced agent would grip far too tightly, Dickens knew, and over commit the machine), and just as it seemed that the cossetting vehicle which had been his protector for that last two hours would become his metal coffin, the nose began to change direction lazily.

Dickens let out a long exhalation and as Mound City flashed by to his right, he let his thoughts return to the morning's events.

The darkness had enveloped the car and was broken only by the twin shafts of light reaching out from either side of the curvaceous bonnet of the car (why did the Americans insist on changing the names of everything? What on earth was a hood? A hood was a criminal, a hoodlum, a crook.) There was not much traffic on the road and what there was ignored the red saloon that was being driven so purposefully.

The mission had been a successful one, three days in and out. He had been required to report at six locations and had performed his duties effectively and efficiently.

Now he had to tidy up the previous mission, which had been left hanging when he had left early in the morning, how many days ago was it? Two? Three?

He glanced in the rear-view mirror and saw that the sun was, if not rising, certainly making its presence felt. The narrow strip of glass appeared as a bronze bracelet, with a verdigris substrata.

He drove on.

This had been over an hour ago, and as he once more flicked his steel eyes towards the mirror he noticed that the sky was now golden: the celestial alchemist had completed his work.

And now he was hungry. Thomas Tom's electronic device showed him that he was fast approaching the old trading post of Rock City, there would be somewhere there for breakfast he mused. It would not be the perfectly cooked soft-boiled eggs, which he had delivered daily from the farm operated by an ex chief petty officer from the Royal Navy, and there would be no wholemeal toast, browned for exactly three minutes and forty-two seconds. The butter would not be the rich jersey butter that he preferred, and the coffee would be a watery liquid which would not deserve to be described in the same breath as the fine blend that he had made up by the Drury Coffee company in the heart of London, and who had been supplying his family for generations.

He knew he had to make many sacrifices in the line of duty, but this? A tall, yellow neon sign which appeared to represent two huge arches, reaching into the sky, was the only beacon of sustenance, and he guided the car into the car park which was filled by huge trucks. The hot metal of the tortured engine clicked as he strode towards the door.

He felt conspicuous in this environment, and wished he had worn a baseball cap this morning, as everyone else here was. He ignored the curious glances that greeted him, and studied the menu with amused interest.

When the waiter, who obstinately remained behind a counter, asked for his order, Dickens said 'I will take one of your Sausage McMuffins, with Egg and you had better make that a meal, I don't want to miss out on the hash brown. I want coffee, hot and strong, and freshly squeezed orange juice. Make it quick, and there will be an extra dollar in it for you!'

The waiter looked at him cautiously, 'what is your name?' he asked.

'Dickens. Gerald Dickens.'

The order came speedily, and Dickens took a seat in a conservatory area and from where he studied the Truck Wash that was situated on a patch of rough ground to the west. From this vantage point he had a wide field of vison, which gave him the maximum opportunity to respond to danger.

The breakfast was surprisingly satisfying, and gave Dickens the boost he needed to face the day. When he had devoured the last scraps of meat and egg, and drained the coffee cup, he returned to the Sonata. Something about that car nagged at him: a memory. What was it? Of course! The Hyundai was made in Korea, and so many years ago he had come face to face with one of his deadliest foes, the mighty force that had been the Oddjob, the Korean henchman of Auric Goldfinger…'

As you will remember from an earlier chapter, the library service was one of my very first venues in 1995 and I have been performing for them ever since and naturally I have built up a good few very special friendships there, particularly Kimberly Howard. When first I performed, Kimberly was a branch librarian at the Blue Springs branch but she rose through the ranks and became head of adult programming, which means that all of my performances for MCPL are planned and produced by her.

Originally my visits allowed me to attend many of the branches of the Library service, but as my following in the Kansas City area grew, so some of the venues became too small and Kimberly sought out alternatives, meaning that many of my largest venues on tour have been in the area, including the massive pyramid structure at the John Knox Pavilion, which can hold a few thousand for music concerts, and around eight hundred for my performances. My audiences here are a particularly loyal group, some members have been coming to my shows since I first performed as a guest from the Dickens Holiday Fair in '95. Indeed, one gentleman not only comes to see me every year, but actually attends every show that I perform at multiple venues and will always stay after the rest of the audience has left for a chat.

The time spent with audiences after a show is always fun, and as the library service does not permit product sales in their venues, the signing sessions can become much more relaxed than at some other stops along the way. I remember once a child was in the line with her mother, and had sat through the whole show. As they reached the desk at which I was sitting, the mother asked 'Now, did you enjoy the play?' 'Yes' replied the girl dutifully. 'Did you have any questions you would like to ask?' prompted the proud parent. The child thought for a while before asking a question that I had never had before, 'Why did you keep talking about spinach?' There was a moment of confusion as we all tried to work out what on earth she was talking about, until it dawned on me – the Spinach of Past, the Spinach of Present and the Spinach of Yet to Come! My diction of the word 'spirit' obviously needed some attention that year.

In my very early years in Missouri I used to travel between events in costume which led to some interesting moments, including a session in a baseball batting gage trying to get bat on a ball fired at me from a pitching machine, whilst resplendent in waistcoat and cravat. On another occasion I was being driven very early one morning to a tiny radio station over the state line in Kansas, it was snowing and the cloud was low, obscuring the view. The station was situated in a small shack at the top of a hill and the overnight snow had left the approach quite treacherous. After a couple of attempts to drive up the hill we realised that it would be impossible, until my driver Marlena noticed that cars had been driving down the hill all morning, leaving that side of the road relatively clear. She announced that we would simply make our way up on the wrong side of the road. I pointed out that this may be somewhat dangerous if a car came over the brow on a collision course with us. It was decided, therefore, that I should walk ahead and signal to any oncoming vehicles that they should stop. I was in frock coat, top hat and scarf, carrying my cane which I could wave to unwary drivers. I made my to the summit and sure enough a pick-up truck driven by a baseball cap wearing man came rumbling towards me, I took off my hat and waved it in one hand, whilst the other scribed great arcs in the cloud with my cane. Can you imagine what the poor driver must have thought? Driving through thick snow he would have suddenly been aware of an apparition of a Victorian gentleman apparently waving in tormented anguish coming out of the mist. If it were in a film the pick-up driver would surely have reached for a bottle of liquor and looked doubtfully at it, before throwing it out of the truck window. Fortunately, he stopped and we made our radio interview unscathed.

Fortin Gage Flowers and Gifts. Nashua, New Hampshire

Since I cut back the number of days that I travel a few years ago, the opportunity for new venues to join the tour have been few and far between, meaning that those who were already on board have an almost permanent place on my schedule.

One sponsor that I have been working with ever since Byers' Choice took over the management of my USA events, is a florist and gift shop based in the heart of downtown Nashua – Fortin Gage. The firm is a family business now run by Jody Gage. The main evening performance used to be held in a large hotel ballroom laid out in a theatre style, meaning that my journey from room to venue was as long as it took for the lift to descend to the ground floor. As in Kansas City the audiences in Nashua are particularly loyal and come to show after show, which means that many of them know the script as well, if not better, than I do! In particular, the scene in which Mrs Cratchit panics about her Christmas pudding is always greeted with hoots of laughter, before I even get to the relevant line. Many has been the time that I have really struggled not to 'corpse' on stage at this point.

From the hotel the show was moved to a college auditorium, which was a wonderful stage to perform on and from there to a very swish country club on the outskirts of the city, and still the audiences followed and still they start to giggle as Mrs Cratchit pauses and says 'Supposin'… 'Supposin'…

But it is not just the mirth of the Cratchits that has made an impression on me in Nashua. For all of the years of performing in the city a certain family – wife, husband and adult son – would attend, and wait quietly after the show until the hustle and bustle of the signing line was over and they could chat. We would talk about my tour (they are keen followers of my blog, so would ask me about things I had written of, whether a cold I had was better or if I had found my fountain pen, or if I'd managed to repair a split costume seam), but one year, very quietly and very solemnly they told me that they had lost a son and wanted me to know that the helplessness and grief with which I performed Bob Cratchit's loss felt completely genuine to them, that they could see themselves in the scene. That evening had a profound effect on me, for it reminded me that you can never completely know who you are performing to or what is going on in their lives. Whenever I reach that scene in the show, the family in Nashua are always in my mind.

Also in Nashua is a Senior Centre and over the last few years Fortin Gage have sponsored a lunchtime event there. Of course, I do not perform A Christmas Carol, for that would take audiences away from my big evening show, so it gives me the opportunity to perform some of my other programmes: Doctor Marigold, The Signalman, Mr Dickens is Coming, Sikes and Nancy and Nicholas Nickleby have all been performed at The Centre over the years, and it has always been an exciting adventure, for the setting for my performance space is not theatrical in any sense – just a large, bare, white room with metal and plastic chairs laid out. As soon as I arrive, an hour before the show, I am greeted by the centre's manager, Judi, and announce 'I need a table, a chair, a screen, a lamp' or whatever that particular show requires and off we go to source the furniture, looking into store cupboards, offices or function rooms. I could of course send my exact requirements ahead of time, but this time has become a fun tradition.

157

Ventfort Hall, Lenox

After many years of looking after my tour Lisa Porter decided to move on to a different company, and so our time of working together came to an end. It was a sad time, for we had worked so closely, and the venues had greatly appreciated Lisa's attention to detail, making sure that the performances went ahead with a minimum of difficulty. When she left, I made Lisa a picture, the frame containing a pen, some cufflinks and a watch, to represent all of the belongings that she had ensured were returned to me over the years.

With Lisa gone it became important to Bob that he found someone else to take over her role, and the answer was close at hand, for his wife Pam stepped up to the plate and has been booking and running my annual tours ever since. The Byers have been good friends for many years, and I have spent Thanksgiving dinners with them and stayed in their house, so Pam was a wonderful choice from my perspective. One of the first new venues that she introduced was a mansion high up in The Berkshires in western Massachusetts, Ventfort Hall in the small town of Lenox.

Driving to Lenox brought back memories of driving to Ojai, for as the journey develops so the scenery becomes more beautiful and the air clearer. I have been treated with snow covered mountain views with clear blue skies behind which are a joy to the soul.

Ventfort Hall was built in the late 19th century as a summer cottage for Sarah Morgan, sister to J Pierpont Morgan (whose fine literary collection included the original handwritten manuscript of *A Christmas Carol*). The Berkshires is a region packed with artists of all disciplines and I received a warm and friendly greeting from all there, but the thing that made the biggest impression on me was the house itself. Made of red brick, it is set slightly back from the road, surrounded by trees. It is not huge and grand in the way that the 'cottages' at Newport, Rhode Island are, but it is obvious that in the Gilded Age it was an impressive and handsome property which has more recently fallen on harder times. The current custodians are working tirelessly to preserve and restore the house, but it is the slightly faded grandeur that appealed to me because it is almost a perfect match to the old school of Ebenezer Scrooge, described by Charles Dickens in the following way:

'They left the high-road, by a well-remembered lane, and soon approached a mansion of dull red brick, with a little weathercock-surmounted cupola, on the roof, and a bell hanging in it. It was a large house, but one of broken fortunes; for the spacious offices were little used, their walls were damp and mossy, their windows broken, and their gates decayed. Fowls clucked and strutted in the stables; and the coach-houses and sheds were over-run with grass. Nor was it more retentive of its ancient state, within; for entering the dreary hall, and glancing through the open doors of many rooms, they found them poorly furnished, cold, and vast. There was an earthy savour in the air, a chilly bareness in the place, which associated itself somehow with too much getting up by candle-light, and not too much to eat.'

As I say, Ventfort is a warm, welcoming place, but that first view on a sunny afternoon as I saw the dull, red brick amongst the trees left a lasting impression on me.

As a theatrical venue Ventfort Hall is similar to the General Crook House in Omaha, as a parlour is converted into a theatre, with the audience squeezed in, and me on a small stage in a bay window. After the performance is finished the audience spread back throughout the hall and dining room of the house where tables have been laid and ready for a beautifully prepared afternoon tea – how very British! While the guests nibble on sandwiches and dainty cakes I stroll from table to table chatting and signing things until it is time for all to drift away into the evening.

The town of Lenox is a historic one with lovely old properties lining its streets, and because my show is an afternoon one, I am always treated to dinner at one of the local restaurants. On my first visit to the town a group of volunteers from Ventfort Hall took me out and we sat in a window seat of a small restaurant on Main Street watching as the snow slowly fell outside, captured in the glittering lights of Christmas decorations. I would not have been surprised, in that moment, to have seen James Stewart gawkily running down the centre of the street shouting out 'Merry Christmas, movie house! Merry Christmas, Emporium! Merry Christmas, you good old Building and Loan!', and it was one of those times in my life when I felt supremely relaxed and happy.

Rogers Gardens, Corona del Mar, California

I rarely get out to the west coast of America these days, but a few years ago Pam was contacted by a large garden centre and plant nursery in California who were interested in scheduling a performance for their guests. During the Christmas season Rogers Gardens features a large Christmas display and carry Byers' Choice merchandise, as well as the Santa figures made by the Vaillancourts (in fact, it was Gary Vaillancourt who convinced the chief byer at Rogers to think about staging a show). When I perform on the east coast during November and December it is easy to imagine that outside the theatre the cold bleak wind is blowing the snow across the earth, but in California the weather is inclined to warm, indeed balmy, and to make the situation even more confusing my shows are held in an open-air amphitheatre in the heart of the complex. The audience sit under large umbrellas, whilst I stride around in thick frock coat, waistcoat, and cravat beneath the blaze of the sun. Lots of sunblock is a necessity when preparing for the show, but as soon as the sweat starts to run off my forehead it gets into my eyes causing them to sting. Not only that but the stage faces to the west, meaning that as the show goes on, so the sun sets lower into the sky causing me to squint – meaning that for most of the performance I have my eyes shut!

But in the evening, when the sky is dark, the stage and auditorium become truly magical. An impressive lighting rig is erected (in fact during my first visit to Rogers the power to the stage was too much and the whole electrical system tripped), and the atmosphere is very cosy, making it much easier to imagine that we are all in London.

Performing at floor level with the audience rising in front of me always reminds me of my early days performing at The Trinity Theatre, and any stage with that configuration brings very happy memories back to me.

The Broad Street United Methodist Church, Burlington, NJ

The United Methodist Church in Burlington New Jersey is another of those venues that transcend the two periods of my touring life, for it was with Caroline that I first visited in 2005. Actually at that time I wasn't performing in the Church itself, but at a huge venue nearby called The Fountain of Life Center, that just happened to have a set built for a production of *A Christmas Carol*. I had great fun using steps and doors and pieces of scenery that had never been available to me before. I seem to remember at one point I exited through a door and then couldn't find my way back onto the stage, creating a moment of panic which I am sure felt much longer to me than it did to the audience.

The Broad Street United Methodist Church itself is a lovely old building, and was dedicated in 1854, the same year that Charles Dickens was working on Hard Times. The sanctuary is a large bright space with a balcony running around three sides. The windows let shafts of sunlight in creating a sense of hope, openness and inclusion. Outside, on Broad Street, a regular tram service rumbles by, and if I get my timing right, the jangling bell can be heard just as I make reference to a church bell ringing in the story, which is always greeted with laughter.

The team at Burlington are wonderful, they are kind and generous and welcoming and go out of their way to put on a good show. For many years the sound was operated by a gentleman called Bob, who sat in the balcony and worked diligently to get the levels just right. Bob's wife Marcia also volunteered to work at the event and would prepare a cup of tea and a plate of biscuits – British Rich Tea biscuits, for me to enjoy in my dressing room. One year I arrived to be greeted by the terribly sad news that Bob had passed away during the year, and there has never been a more poignant moment in any of my shows than when I got to the end of the performance and said 'Nooooo Bob' I looked up to the balcony where he had sat in previous years and bowed my head a little out of respect to a kind, gentle man.

Winterthur

In the heart of The Brandywine Valley close to the state line between Delaware and Pennsylvania the grand house and gardens of Winterthur nestle in the hills. Winterthur was built by the DuPont family at around the same times as Charles Dickens was enjoying his early successes and would become the home of Henry Francis DuPont, who delighted in collecting American antiques and art.

Nowadays Winterthur is open to the public, who spend hours roaming the gardens and exploring the house dreaming of a golden age, of living in such luxury and grandeur.

As my 'Byer's Choice era' tour developed, Winterthur made enquiries for me to perform there, not in the house itself but in a lecture theatre attached to the modern visitor centre a short walk away, and it is that lecture theatre that is the true star of the show at Winterthur. It is a long room, seating around four hundred with a low stage at the front.

First visits to any venue can be awkward as you greet people you have never met before and try to work out how the show will work. One of the first jobs is to perform a sound check, hoping that the microphone and amplification system will be a good one (not always the case, and stories of various amplification malfunctions could fill another book). At Winterthur, looking at the rows of seats disappearing into the darkness, I particularly hoped that everything would work, or half the audience wouldn't hear a thing. I clipped the microphone on, walked onto the stage and began reciting the words of the show: 'Marley was dead, to begin with!' Except that is not what I heard, instead the hall was filled with 'Marley Marley Marley Marley was was was was dead dead dead dead...' the echoes reverberated through the room coming back to me and told me everything that I needed to know about the Copeland Hall, it had a perfect acoustic. I have never used a microphone at Winterthur, for the barrel-roof construction of the building makes the whole space a microphone. I don't even need to project very much to let every member of the audience hear my words, it is an amazing room and architects of modern performance spaces could learn a lot from a visit to Winterthur. Mind you, every year I stand on the stage and look out into the auditorium, and every year I doubt that my voice can actually carry to the back wall, but it always does.

Soon Winterthur was a regular feature on my schedule and the staff, volunteers and audience members became good friends and colleagues. My 'dressing room' was actually a tiny office which was the domain of Barbara, the manager of the large and thriving retail store. It was always a lovely feeling to dip into somebody else's 'life' for a short while, for Barbara had a huge collection of little cartoons pinned to her notice boards, and there were other notices too, about the running of the business, that nobody but the employees would understand - a sort of secret code. I always liked 'Deposit slips only have three pieces rather than four. No more blue, so send Jenn the PINK copy' and was very sorry when one year I discovered a new system in place and that notice removed. I felt sorry that Jen, whoever she was, didn't now just need the PINK copy.

Winterthur also mounted some wonderful special exhibitions, including superbly curated displays of costumes from Downton Abbey and, later, from The Crown, which always made the place feel very British – a home from home.

There are many other venues I could talk about and describe, and I have special memories from each and every one – of the buildings, the people, or about things that have happened during my performances. My life on the road has been an amazing one and it has never felt routine, or a burden. Each time I stand at the edge of the stage ready to begin, whether that is in the dark of a large theatre or in the bright light of a simple meeting room, I get the same frisson of excitement, the same sense of adventure, as I did when I first read *A Christmas Carol* in 1993.

Chapter 9
Acting Notes

As the new era of touring began so many more of my performances became theatre-style events, rather than being squeezed around a formal dinner, and it was during this period that I really started to work harder on the finer details of the show. From being a slightly slapstick romp through the story, I began to consider the finer details and to capture the exact atmosphere that Charles Dickens had created in 1843. Although I have never formally had a director on the show, I have been greatly assisted over the years by Liz, who sees the performance maybe once or twice a year and therefore can see the changes that I have made. If there are issues or things that can be improved, she will very gently mention them to me. Sometimes I rail against what she says and then quietly reflect on the suggestion and inevitably will include them during future performances.

The other source of direction comes from my audiences, many of whom seem to know the show better than I do. The show will gently develop during a tour and the constant experimenting keeps it fresh for me. Although the skeleton of the show does not change much, the little changes and tweaks I make can mean that the 'feeling', the atmosphere can be different. An audience member who watches the show keenly will not have seen the performance for twelve months, by which time it has undergone a full cycle of changes. After one show during my 2018 tour a gentleman came up to me during a signing session and said 'I don't want to criticise, but I felt you were a bit too hurried, in particular the snoring. Usually you pause before you snore, but today you went straight into it!'

In this chapter I want to share with you how I perform my current show. This is being written in the Spring of 2023 and by the time you watch me things may have changed such is the constant evolution, but for now this is how I have adapted and how I perform *A Christmas Carol*.

Throughout this description I shall use the theatrical terms for various positions on the stage: downstage is closest to the audience, upstage is at the back, right and left are from the actor's point of view as he looks at the audience.

Stave 1: Marley's Ghost

The stage is set simply: a chair is positioned upstage right, with a red cloth draped over it. There is a hat stand beside it. Downstage left is a simple wooden stool. For the opening of the show this will represent Scrooge's counting house – the chair representing the office and the stool Bob Cratchit's desk. At the back of the stage is a table, with a simple candlestick on it.

For a costume I wear a generic Victorian-style frock coat, grey, high-waisted trousers (secured with buttoned braces), a bright red and gold waistcoat, that has a festive feel to it and a burgundy cravat. The frock coat can be buttoned up so that in certain scenes the waistcoat is hidden. I have a top hat, a thick scarf and carry a simple wooden walking cane.

The first decision I had to make in preparing the script was how to actually begin the show, and over the years I have tried three different versions. However, they all have in common the use the first lines of the book itself: 'Marley was dead, to begin with…' Can there be a better opening than that?

My first opening was simple, I stood in the centre of the stage and talking directly to the audience, said: 'A Christmas Carol' by Charles Dickens. Stave 1 Marley's Ghost: Marley was dead, to begin with…' This worked well enough, but it lacked a sense of drama , the show sort of just began without anyone really noticing, so I decided to change the beginning to use the preface that Charles Dickens had attached to the original edition: 'I have endeavoured in this Ghostly little book to raise the Ghost of an idea, which shall not put my readers out of humour with themselves, with each other, with the season, or with me. May it haunt their houses pleasantly, and no one wish to lay it. 'A Christmas Carol'. Stave 1, Marley's Ghost. Marley was dead to begin with…' In this way I cast myself in the character of Charles Dickens reading to a captive audience, and therein lay the problem – I didn't want the show to be seen as a reading (in fact I actively discourage venues from using the 'R' work in any marketing), I wanted a more theatrical opening.

The most recent version of the start came to me one day as I listened to my Christmas playlist in a dressing room before a show. One of my favourite tracks is 'Christmas Eve. Sarajevo 12/24' by the Trans-Siberian Orchestra. It is a haunting piece of music and would immediately create a mournful atmosphere for the mournful opening to the book. I took the idea to a local sound engineer who lifted the opening bars (before the heavy rock kicks in) and then added the sound of a heavy church bell tolling. Instantly the audience would be transported into an eerie churchyard. In a theatre setting I decided to make my entrance as the music played not as myself, but in the character of Ebenezer Scrooge walking behind Jacob Marley's coffin, the coat is buttoned up and the scarf wrapped around his neck. As the last toll of the bell fades away I look away from the imaginary grave and at the audience: 'Marley was dead, to begin with...' I had found the theatricality and drama that I had been searching for over the years.

The opening of *A Christmas Carol* is all about scene-setting, narrative, and establishing the character of old Ebenezer. I have already quoted the description of Scrooge that enabled me to physically become his character, but there are important subtleties in these passages that are vital to the success and believability of the entire story. Scrooge is not a villain; he is not a bad man. Charles Dickens goes to great length to point out that his offices are in the heart of the City of London: 'on 'change' refers to the Royal Exchange which is situated close to the Bank of England, so Ebenezer is not some back-street money lender, he is a respected and respectful businessman. His voice and demeanour must reflect his status, so I use a well-to-do London accent with a very definite and assured delivery.

Within these opening passages I also introduce a device that hopefully will put the audience at ease with the show – showing them that it is OK to laugh and join in. In the original novel Dickens breaks away from a traditional style of narrative, almost talking to the reader as if he is sitting next to them. Having created the mystery of the opening scene, I suddenly break character, and the fourth wall, by saying: 'Mind! I don't mean to say that I know what there is particularly dead about a door–nail. Do you? I might have been inclined, myself, to regard a coffin–nail as the deadest piece of ironmongery in the trade, would you agree? Good, because it is in the book! But the wisdom of our ancestors is in the simile; and my unhallowed hands shall not be allowed to disturb it, or the Country's done for.

'So, you will therefore permit me to repeat, emphatically, that Marley was as dead as a... door–nail.' And I encourage the audience to join in with the final word, meaning that they are not only watching the show but are now involved in it too.

After using the book's narrative and my musical sound effect to create a mysterious, dark, cold atmosphere, the tone changes with the arrival of Scrooge's nephew. One of the nice things about adapting the original text is that even if a passage doesn't actually feature in my script, it can still exist in the performance. Dickens' words become the greatest stage directions ever written, and although I don't say the following words, they are certainly present in the show:

'He had so heated himself with rapid walking in the fog and frost, this nephew of Scrooge's, that he was all in a glow; his face was ruddy and handsome; his eyes sparkled, and his breath smoked again.' As I bound across the stage in the character of Fred I make sure that the frock coat is unbuttoned, so that the audience get a flash of the gold and red waistcoat which has been hidden up until now.

The dialogue between Fred and Ebenezer bounces back and forth with great pace, so it is vital that the audience understand who is talking at any given point. Obviously, there is a vocal difference between the two characters, but this is the perfect moment in the script to establish a way of showing two separate individuals on the same stage at the same time: it is a simple matter of eye contact.

For example, Fred is more mobile than his uncle, so as he speaks, he is usually pacing around the stage. If we imagine

Scrooge standing in the centre, then Fred needs to be looking towards that point, turning his head as he moves thus maintaining eye contact. When old Ebenezer answers it is essential that he looks to the last place from where Fred has delivered his line, as if speaking directly to him. It is even possible to convince the audience that the invisible character is on the move by letting the speaker follow him with his eyes. It is also important for me to establish the height of each character, Fred being slightly taller. So that Scrooge has to look up a little when berating his nephew.

Fred is replaced by the charity collector, whose character changes during the course of the scene under the onslaught of Scrooge. He begins as a kindly, caring, liberal gentleman who naturally assumes that everybody must share his concerns about the plight of the poor. He starts his scene with a well-rehearsed speech, quoting statistics and preparing to receive a sizeable donation. As it is late in the day, we may assume that the gentleman has visited many offices throughout Christmas Eve, and equally we may assume that his quest has met with considerable success, so when Scrooge answers his enquiry with a stark, bold 'NOTHING', he is shocked. Briefly he believes that he has misunderstood, and that Scrooge just wants to remain anonymous, but the old man makes it quite clear that he wishes 'to be left alone'. The prepared script is now useless, and the gentleman's real nature shines through, in response to Ebenezer's assertion that he pays for the prisons and workhouses out of his taxes (another hint from Dickens that old Scrooge is a law-abiding citizen), and those in need should go there, the collector replies that 'many can't go there, many would rather die' 'If they would rather die', replies Scrooge, 'then perhaps they had better do it and decrease the surplus population! Good afternoon, sir.'

Originally, I delivered that final speech in an angry tone with the final three words shouted as Ebenezer slammed the door shut behind the poor gent. However, in recent years, I have found that the lines have much more impact delivered from Scrooge's chair, with the old man scarcely even acknowledging the tormented individual. Scrooge has moved on and is back to work, swatting the charity collected way as he may an annoying insect. This delivery was inspired by that of George C Scott in the 1984 film adaptation of *A Christmas Carol,* one of my favourites.

One final point about the charity collector, and that is where my inspiration for his voice and demeanour came from. He is one of the characters who still has the same voice as the one I used for my very first reading in 1993, and it came from an unlikely source: the former Prime Minister, Margaret Thatcher. In television interviews Mrs Thatcher would sometimes attempt to show a caring side, not always successfully, and would tilt her head to one side and affect a soothing tone, almost a whisper. The most memorable time that she did this was when she announced the birth of her first grandchild with the words 'we are a grandmother' as if she were the Monarch, and in those four words was born the charity collector!

As an actor I do like to know the background of a character and to understand their motivations. In recent years the collector (or collectors as they are in the novel), has confused me. Surely if he is local, he must know that Scrooge would not donate and that any attempt to reason with him would be doomed to failure, so I have come to the conclusion that he is new in town and maybe colleagues at the charity have played a prank on him and suggested he visits Scrooge and Marley. Of course, ultimately the joke will be turned, for only a few hours later old Scrooge will run up to the man offering him a huge donation. I imagine him going back to the office and smugly telling the others 'Old Scrooge, not so difficult, just needed a bit of charm!'

Back to the show, and the story continues. After the charity collector leaves, I have included a line that although not necessary from a storytelling point of view, is a reminder to the audience of the claustrophobic and ghostly atmosphere outside. After two scenes of dialogue the simple line 'Foggier yet, and colder! Piercing, biting cold' is delivered slowly and portentously to create that feeling.

I don't use many sound effects in the show, but if I did, I would love the slow ticking of a clock during the next moments. In the dark office Scrooge and his clerk work on to the end of the working day, only briefly interrupted by the visit of a carol singer who is sent running by Ebenezer. When the time to close the office comes Ebenezer summons Cratchit to discuss the arrangements for Christmas day. For many years I had Scrooge look at his watch before commanding the clerk to his office: 'Cratchit. Here!', but in the novel Bob Cratchit is never mentioned by name (indeed neither are the nephew or the charity collector, it is as if nobody exists as individuals in Scrooge's world, simply as functionaries), so I amended the line to simply 'You. Here!'

Bob Cratchit's physical character is entirely of my invention and has no background in the novel. I wanted him to be a complete opposite to Scrooge. Ebenezer is direct and firm, so Cratchit had to be nervous and unsure. Scrooge barks his words confidently, whereas Cratchit hesitates and stutters. Scrooge's gestures are strong, so Cratchit's are weak. To complete this contrast, I decided to give Bob a very soft accent, to contrast with the harsh London tones of Scrooge. Originally, I had wanted to make Cratchit Welsh, as that accent is one of the gentlest, most lyrical, beautiful accents in the British Isles, but I soon discovered that I couldn't hold it, so instead settled on an accent from Cornwall, in the far West of England. As I mentioned, in the novel there is no hint that the Cratchit family hailed from anywhere other than Camden Town, but in my show they have come to London from Cornwall.

When Bob has finally been dismissed, he joyfully runs home and plays Blindman's Buff with his family, which I mime, and the first 'figure' that he stumbles upon is represented by the wooden hatstand, at which point I can transform myself back into Scrooge collecting his hat and scarf and buttoning his coat up again before walking from his office and out into the snow (represented by huddling into the scarf and bending forward as if walking into a heavy wind).

The route around the stage takes Scrooge back to the stool that had previously represented Bob Cratchit's work station, but by sitting down and facing towards the stage right wing, instead of forwards, it is now a chair in the melancholy tavern where Ebenezer takes his melancholy dinner. As he sits I mine first turning the page of a broadsheet newspaper, and then focussing on a tiny notebook, his banker's book, at which he gives a little chuckle.

Having finished his meal Ebenezer stands, puts on his hat and walks to his apartments, the imaginary door to which is situated to the centre of the stage. By holding up my top hat to face the audience, and resting the handle of my walking cane against it, I create the image of the famous door knocker. Continuing the narrative, I turn as I speak so that the hat is now covering my face and at the moment that Marley's face appears, I lower that hat revealing my face which represents not only the death mask of Jacob, but also shows the shock and horror of Ebenezer.

If I am in a theatre with adjustable lighting, I will have arranged for a spot light to be focussed just on the face giving it the eerie glow 'like a bad lobster in a dark cellar', that Dickens describes. With the line '…it was a knocker again,' the hat comes back up and after a slight pause I peer around it anxiously as if not quite believing what has just happened.

The knocker
Photo Credit: Ian Dickens

As Scrooge trudges his way upstairs the narrative tells us that he is trimming his candle as climbs, and I have often experimented with using an actual candlestick which is on the upstage table. From entering the door, I walk to the table, pick up the candle and then slowly make my way downstage again. On the line 'darkness is cheap, Scrooge liked it' I blow the candle out, leaving a little whisp of smoke in the air. This solution isn't perfect for I end up putting the candlestick back in the same spot I have taken it from. If Bob Cratchit had an actual desk (and I own a suitable clerk's desk which I use in my performance of The Signalman), then there would be no problem, but such a large piece of furniture would dominate the front of the stage and get in the way of later scenes, so that is not an option. Once Ebenezer is upstairs, and before retiring for the night, he makes a nervous search of his rooms. It was during this scene that one of many happy accidents occurred when a moment of inspiration led me to improvise a movement. Many years ago, right at the start of my touring life, I decided that it might be fun to make the dressing gown hanging on the wall a character in its own right. By standing at the back, rising myself on my toes and dropping a shoulder and letting my dangling arms swing ever so slightly, as if in a breeze, I transform myself into a simple fabric garment dangling from a hook. This simple movement provoked a wonderful laugh from the audience, and it has remained in the show ever since.

Now the clanking of Jacob Marley's chains comes up the stairs and towards the door. The process is illustrated by an outstretched arm, hand and finger pointing forward, every muscle tensed and strong. The focus of my eyes is directly down the arm, thereby creating an incredibly strong and powerful image, which sends Scrooge back onto his knees cowering in fear.

Charles Dickens tells us a great deal about Jacob Marley and all of this information can be collated to create the character on stage. Firstly, and somewhat obviously, he is dead, so his movements need to be slightly other-worldly. He is weighed down by heavy chains, which restrict his movements, making his progress somewhat ponderous, although I try also to introduce a lightness and weightlessness to his progress.

Another clue as to my representation of Jacob lies within the text, when he tells Scrooge that 'I cannot rest, I cannot stay, I cannot linger anywhere,' meaning that I ensure that is never for a moment still, he is always pacing as he speaks. Even during Ebenezer's dialogue, I make sure that he is addressing his words to a constantly moving figure.

Assuming that a ghost, especially one with 'death-cold eyes', cannot see in a conventional sense, I purposefully avoid actual eye contact between Jacob and Ebenezer, the ghostly face gazing off into the sky, even though many of his gestures are directed towards Ebenezer.

As to a voice, Jacob's conversation is later described as being 'dull' so his speech is delivered in monotone with little cadence to it. There is anguish and torture behind his words and also a sense that he doesn't know when he will move on and away, meaning that he must keep talking before it is too late.

The scene with Jacob Marley only holds one purpose within the telling of the story, and that is to inform Scrooge – and us – that he is to be taken on a journey (of course, within Marley's soliloquies there are wonderful observations about the plight of society and the terrible gap between rich and poor, but they do not further the plot as such), and there is only one line that really matters: 'You will be haunted by three spirits, without their visits you cannot hope to shun the path I tread.' Naturally, it would be sacrilege to cut the scene that drastically, but it is important to get Scrooge into the real action of the story, so I have edited out a lot of the original dialogue, although each year I relent and re-introduce a little more! When I extended the show to become a two-act performance it was mainly in the Jacob Marley scene that the extra material was added, and I was grateful for the opportunity to do so.

As Marley comes to the end of his visit he walks slowly backwards up stage, and if I time it right by the time he delivers his final line I am against the back wall – sometimes in a theatre the back of the stage will be a large, heavy black curtain and as Marley floats '… into the bleak, dark night' I can grab the curtains to create a large wave effect as if the very fabric of space has been agitated. Ebenezer is left alone in the room before collapsing in exhaustion and falling into an uneasy sleep on the chair, which now represents his bed, pulling the red cloth over him as if it were his blanket, and falling into a sleep which is represented by gentle snoring. At one point I cry out 'Jacob! Old Jacob…' as if he is having a nightmare about his long dead business partner.

Stave 2: The First of the Three Spirits
When Scrooge comes face to face with the first ghost is it not an easy entity to portray: '… being now a thing with one arm, now with one leg, now with twenty legs, now a pair of legs without a head, now a head without a body…' Not all together helpful to an actor, and it is no surprise that the Ghost of Christmas Past is the only one not illustrated in the original book.

I chose to play the ghost as an ethereal, androgynous entity, and its movements are floating and gentle as though its ever-changing form consists of diaphanous fabrics which are stirred by the slightest breeze. The voice is equally without form and is, for the most part, a high monotone (slightly therefore mirroring that of Jacob Marley). The spirit takes Ebenezer by the hand and as a performer it is vital to establish their respective heights. In the form of Scrooge my hand is held low and speech is directed downward, and as the spirit I look back and up. But, despite the tiny stature of the ghost it is obvious where the strength lies, so Scrooge is pulled along, helplessly.

The opening dialogue leaves Scrooge in no doubt that the ghost is in charge, there is a sense of no choice as to whether Ebenezer should go or not, so the tone has to be firm. This first encounter is one of the most important in the book, for Scrooge's ultimate reformation begins here, back on the road to his old school, seeing his old friends and 'recognising every gate, every post, and tree'.

For the story to work every single thing that Scrooge is shown by the three spirits must make a difference to him. I have seen stage shows in which Ebenezer remains irascible throughout the entire performance until he is terrified by the vision of his future and death, which doesn't make any sense at all.

In my version, Scrooge's entire demeanour – even his way of moving - lightens as they pass through the wall together and he is like a child again as he runs along the road (it is a movement that is echoed at the end of the story: 'I am as merry as a schoolboy!')

It is when Scrooge sees his young self, sat alone in the schoolroom, that the gravity of his life first becomes apparent to him. Sorrowfully he says 'poor boy' and then, as he takes a Victorian penny from his waistcoat pocket and looks towards the area of the stage where his counting house door had been in scene one, he repeats the line. The repetition does not feature in the book, but I wanted Scrooge to feel sorry for himself and realise that the full significance of how he has treated others. As he looks at the coin he thinks about the carol singer that he had sent packing the previous evening and whispers (more to himself, than to the spirit) 'I would have liked to have been able to give him a little something...' And the change within him has begun.

From the schoolroom to the warehouse door, and the weight of the previous scene is lifted. I take the chance of an expansive entry into the scene to unbutton my coat once more so that a splash of colour is injected into the proceedings. The stage is filled with the sheer joy of Mr Fezziwig in all his energetic delight. My character of Scrooge's old employer is based entirely on John Leech's original illustration, for how can you not look at that picture without smiling. The first edition of the book featured five coloured prints and seven other engravings, and I have tried to capture the exact pose of each throughout the show.

Everything about the Fezziwig scene should be happy and bathed in a warm rosy glow. When the order is given to tidy the warehouse so there is a blur as Dick Wilkins and young Mr Scrooge obey, but within this moment two very important things take place: firstly the stool that has sat at the front of the stage since the opening of the show is replaced to the back, next to the little table, whilst the red cloth on the chair that had been a bed cover flung aside, is apparently carelessly folded, but in fact carefully rolled with more cloth at one end, giving it the appearance of a swaddled baby, after which it is laid back across the arm of the chair, unnoticed.

'In came a fiddler and went up to the lofty desk, and made

an orchestra of it, and tuned like fifty stomach aches,' is one of the book's most wonderful lines, and in my show, I leap onto the chair, now representing that lofty desk, and screech a few tuneless notes. Down to the floor again and a quick description of the feast laid out for the revellers before Mr and Mrs Fezziwig stand out to dance. It has only been in recent years that I have introduced sound effects and music into the show, and I use them sparingly, but at this point the sound of a fiddler playing the English country dance Sir Roger de Coverley fills the hall. In the persona of Mr and Mrs F I skip, twirl, advance and retreat until the dance reaches its climax with Mrs Fezziwig in a slightly awkward and unbalanced spinning pirouette. I can't dance. I don't like to dance. I do not feel comfortable dancing, but at Fezziwig's ball the sheer joy of the occasion becomes contagious, and on occasion I even receive an impromptu round of applause for my efforts.

As the scene fades away, Scrooge again becomes reflective and when the ghost asks what he is thinking about, he replies that he would like to say a word or two to his clerk. As he says this, I make sure that he is positioned at the very point where Bob's stool had been. He gestures towards the spot but realises that the stool has disappeared – it is almost as if he has lost the opportunity to make amends with Bob.

One little touch that I have included in this scene is for Scrooge to mention Bob's name for the first time in the story, and it is a struggle for him to remember it.

From the old warehouse we are suddenly in another place and time, Scrooge has grown slightly older now and is sat next his fiancé Belle, his coat formally buttoned up once more. In the book this is quite a long scene as Belle explains her sadness and disappointment at Scrooge, whereas he rationalises his tardiness in planning a wedding by discussing the fragility of his business interests. In the show I have condensed this scene into a few lines, but the upshot is the same as she sorrowfully releases Ebenezer from their engagement. As she leaves, she turns, pulling an imaginary ring from her finger and throws it back at him. The young Scrooge commands her to 'come back, don't go…' but even as I am saying it, I change my voice from young to old and it is now a distraught Ebenezer pleading with his younger self 'go after her, man, don't let her go. As he calls out, the words of the spirit come back to him: 'these are the shadows of things that have been they will have no consciousness of us,' and his voice falters as he repeats 'don't… let… her… go.'

And so Scrooge is broken. The spirit has achieved everything it set out to do and surely has nothing more to offer, but the pain is not yet finished, and maybe this is the cruellest thing that the Ghost of Christmas Past does: for there is Belle again, happy, married, content, sitting opposite her beautiful daughter. Life has moved on for her, but Scrooge is left trembling and crying as he watches, thinking of what might have – what should have – been.

The husband arrives – Scrooge does not know him, which only strengthens the idea that she is now living in a completely different world. I play the scene for laughs at first, for Belle answers her husband's comment that he had seen an old friend of hers in a rather silly and flighty manner, but when she realises who he is talking about her voice changes: 'Not… not Mr Scrooge?' She is overwhelmed with remorse, guilt, but ultimately with a deeply held affection. Absentmindedly she twists the Wedding ring on her finger, but she is thinking of the engagement ring that she had thrown away so many years before.

The revelation that old Marley is now lying on the point

of death, and that Scrooge is quite alone in the world is hardly important to old Ebenezer, for from the depths of his misery, there is a chink of light: Belle had remembered him.

I close the scene by recreating another of the Leech illustrations, as Scrooge forces a giant candle snuffer over the ghost's figure, thereby extinguishing its light forever. Alone on the stage, Scrooge looks about him and sees that he is crouching on the floor of his own room, and with that he returns to the chair and is soon snoring loudly once more.

Stave Three: The Second of the Three Spirits
If I am performing a two act show, the first lines of the second act are delivered from the darkness and they are an echo of Jacob Marley's warning 'You will be haunted by three spirits. Expect the first tonight when the bell tolls one, expect the second on the next night at the same hour.' The lights come up to reveal Scrooge sleeping soundly on the chair, snoring loudly until he wakes with a start.

The arrival of the second ghost is shrouded in mystery, for although the clock is striking one there is no spirit in his room and it is not for a further fifteen minutes that Scrooge realises that his next visitor is in fact in the adjoining room. The appearance of The Ghost of Christmas Present is another moment taken from the original Leech artwork, I stand proudly, left arm outstretched looking down towards the terrified figure of Scrooge who, in turn, looks upward with his hands held together as if in prayer

Another source of inspiration for the ghost's appearance is taken from a production of *A Christmas Carol* performed by the Missouri Rep Theatre Company in Kansas City: the ghost was fired through the stage trap door and burst into the scene like a space rocket, accompanied by bright light and billowing smoke. When he landed perfectly, balletically, on his feet we saw that he was a very tall figure in full Rastafarian regalia with his Rasta cap and dreadlocks. Never has the line, 'You have never seen the like of me before', been more appropriate. In my show I try to create the same sense of fun and shock by striking a one-legged pose as he says the line.

The Ghost of Christmas Present
Photo Credit: Phil Hinton

The Ghost is a giant and every movement is large and expansive, every gesture bold and defined. For a voice he has a broad Yorkshire accent, and exudes charm and openness, in fact he is everything that Scrooge is not. Despite himself Scrooge enjoys the ghost's company, and even permits himself a smile, as they exchange pleasantries. Scrooge's words are very important here, he says 'I went forth last night, upon compulsion, and I learned a lesson that is working for me now. Tonight, if you have ought to show me, let me profit by it.' Even at this early stage in his journey he is aware that the ghosts are visiting for his own good, and despite the pain and anguish of his time in the past, he recognises the lesson it taught, so he is anxious to go with the ghost, he wants to learn and certainly doesn't fight against it.

For the journey through the streets of London I take the character of the Ghost, striding around the stage as if through a tiny model village, Scrooge somewhere in his wake. Along the way he describes people on Christmas morning being in such a hurry that they 'tumble up against one another' and over the years this has been a line where I can have some fun. In the days when I was performing in hotel dining rooms I would leave the stage and walk between tables and at the perfect moment would feign tripping over an outstretched leg or a pushed-back chair. From my sprawled position on the floor, I would come out of character and dress down the poor individual I had chosen, pointing out that they had brought the whole show to a shuddering halt by tripping me. Then, almost seamlessly, I returned to the narrative '… but when there were angry words between them, the ghost shed a few drops of water on them from his torch and their good humour was restored directly. For they said, 'It's a shame to quarrel upon Christmas Day!' And so it was. God love it, so it was' at which point I would shake them warmly by the hand, and continue on my way.

On the stage, rather than in a dining room, I play the scene by tripping over my own ankle, as if colliding with another person, and then turn to take up boxer's pose, fists clenched, and arm drawn back as if to deliver a quick right jab (If the time of year is right, I take a moment to deliver an aside to the audience, 'It's like Black Friday!' or comparing the situation to the local shopping mall, before letting the scene play on). The action freezes mid-pose and I become the ghost, striding around the pugilists and holding his hand high as if dripping the water from his torch, I then let my body resume the fighting stance once more, which in turn melts as the characters realise the foolishness of their attitude, shake hands and walk off into the crowd the best of friends.

The Spirit marches through the town to Bob Cratchit's house, which is situated to the left side of the stage, and as they enter, I bend my head slightly, as if the giant must squeeze in at a low window. The first member of the family we see is Mrs Cratchit, and her 'tick' is to be constantly wiping her hands on an apron (the skirt of my frock coat). She is a bundle of nerves and despite looking after her children, is trying to prepare for the great Christmas feast, she is looking here and there at this pan and that pot. Her main concern though is for her husband Bob and Tiny Tim. Soon however, they arrive, Bob rushing in, and on his shoulder he holds the red cloth that was so carefully prepared back in the Fezziwig scene to represent the frail figure of Tim. The idea to use a cloth in this way was Liz's and she first suggested it having seen me perform Doctor Marigold in which the main character similarly holds a child on his shoulder. I mimed cradling the little creature but somehow it didn't work, so Liz said 'why not actually physically hold something, and suggested I had a blanket on the set that could rolled into a suitable shape. The effect worked so well for Marigold that we adopted it for *A Christmas Carol* too. The wooden walking cane, that I use throughout the show, now represents Tim's crutch, and is perfect for the job for it is rustic and gnarled and basic.

The Cratchit scene is another that has lengthened over the years and now I include the short dialogue between the couple regarding Tiny Tim at church, the cloth is carefully laid on the little table, whilst the crutch is propped up against the wooden stool, thus creating a little Tiny Tim Tableau.

Soon the dinner is served and thanks to the luscious description provided by Charles Dickens, delivered with loving detail by me, hopefully the audience's mouths are watering along

Bob Cratchit and Tiny Tim
Photo Credit: Phil Hinton

with those of the Cratchit children. Typically, I will describe the preparation of the potatoes, the apple sauce and then the gravy, and as I talk about the murmur of delight arising around the table, I gently gesture to the left-hand side of the audience, encouraging them to join in, which (hopefully) they do not. In mock frustration I go to the other side of the audience and repeat the line, at which of course everyone joins in the 'ahhhhhhhhhh'. Having berated the left side of the audience,

('It's too late now! I am going to take my goose over here now…') I concentrate on the right-hand bank of the audience for the rest of the show the Cratchit family is in the stage right position.

I don't remember where this audience participation scene first came from, I imagine I used to approach a dining table in one of the large hotels and invited them to be the Cratchit family and when they didn't play ball, moved on to another, but, however, it started it has become a favourite part of the show now. It has been interesting to see how regular audiences approach this scene: those who really know the show understand that to NOT react is the correct thing to do, those who are at venues where I have perhaps visited two or three times think that they should join in with the first 'AAAAHHHHH' which completely throws me, as I have to quickly change the movements for the rest of the show!

Straight after the goose comes the scene in which Mrs Cratchit fetches the Christmas Pudding from the wash house. I have already described the very real concern that my mother felt about the cooking of The Christmas Pudding, so Mrs Cratchit's panics are rooted in genuine fear.

Standing downstage right of the stage and addressing the audience as if they are her family she asks: 'Supposin'… 'supposin' it should not be done enough. EEK!' and she runs for the to the door (upstage left), before a new fear envelops her. She returns to her original spot: 'supposin… supposin' it should break in the turning out. EEK!' Again, she runs to the door before yet another wave of fear grips her. She returns downstage once more, this time barely able to speak, 'Supposin'… supposin… that somebody should have climbed across the wall and stolen it! AGGGGHHHHHHH!' and she runs off the stage screaming loudly, and you can almost see her skirt, apron and cloth billowing behind her.

The repetition and the timing of the scene builds the

humorous tension to near breaking point. At venues where I have been performing for many years the laughter often starts before I have even said the first words, and it sometimes difficult for me to keep a straight face.

Of course, the pudding is pronounced perfect, and the rest of the feast passes off joyfully. But there now comes a change in the tone of the storytelling, from being a fun-loving, gregarious, rumbustious figure, the Ghost of Christmas Present suddenly becomes a threatening and portentous entity who not only chastises but also taunts Scrooge.

I have developed a bit of business with the cane during this exchange, which helps show the dominant and submissive roles taken by the ghost and Scrooge in the scene. When Scrooge asks if Tiny Tim will live, the ghost gestures toward the empty stool with the wooden cane propped against it (unless it has fallen over which does sometimes happen), and then sweeps it up into his hand and holds it high above his head as he barks 'I see a vacant seat in the poor chimney corner, and a crutch without an owner, carefully preserved' at which he drops the cane as if carelessly discarding it. As the cane falls towards the floor, I drop to my knees and am now the in the character of Scrooge cowering penitently, and he is able to catch the cane. 'No, no, say the child will be spared' and he holds the cane up as if it is an offering. The ghost snatches it in his hand, and I stand tall and powerful once more to deliver the next line: 'If these shadows remain unaltered by the Future, the child will die. What then? If he be like to die, then perhaps he had better do it, and decrease the surplus population.' And with that he drops, almost throws, the cane down once more with great finality. If I am performing on a raised stage I try to perform this moment right at the very edge, so that the cane is dropped into an apparent abys and Scrooge (back crouching again), actually catches it below the level of the floor, as if reaching down into Tiny Tim's grave. His head is bowed as he listens to the ghost's final words, and slowly makes his way to replace the cane against the stool.

With my back to the audience, I now break into cheerful laughter, which is cut short as I, as Scrooge, turn my head to look inquisitively at what is happening, but there is nothing to see, so he turns back to the stool again, at which the shriek of laughter resumes and he turns quickly again. We are now in his nephew's house and the claustrophobic intensity of the previous scene has gone, instead the stage is awash with joy, 'there is nothing in the world so irresistibly contagious as laughter and good humour!' For a long time this line was one of those silent 'stage directions', but its eventual inclusion was inevitable and as of Christmas 2021 it became a permanent part of the script.

The scene is Fred's party and the characters are in high spirts, giggling together about old Scrooge's refusal to join them on Christmas day. This is another scene in which a great deal of information from the novel needs to be communicated in short space of time, the most important thing being that Ebenezer is ultimately defended by his nephew. The discussion about Scrooge passes in a moment as the guests forget all about him and play a game of blind man's buff, and here we meet the lascivious, flirtatious, seductive cad, Topper. Many audience members think that I have created and included this scene for comic effect, but it is lifted straight out of the 1843 text. My rendition of Topper is based on a mixture of two British actors, both of whom made their names in comedy films made during the 1950s and 60s, Terry Thomas and Leslie Phillips. Topper's greeting of 'Well, hello!' could come from either of them, although the style is more that of

Phillips whose catchphrase, when his character saw a pretty girl, was 'Ding Dong!'

Blindman's Buff ends up with Topper catching the object of his affections and they cuddle together behind the curtains (me standing with my back to the audience with my arms wrapped around myself, as if in a warm and private embrace).

The scene is soon over, and the travellers continue on their way. This is a section of the book that I do not capture effectively, for the actual passage takes Scrooge and the ghost down mines, over cliffs, out to sea, into lighthouses, and everywhere Christmas is being honoured and celebrated, it is a wonderful piece of prose but in my show it is reduced to, 'Much they saw, and far they went, and many homes they visited, but always with a happy end. The Spirit stood beside sick beds, and they were cheerful; on foreign lands, and they were close at home; by poverty, and it was rich.' The whirlwind nature of their journey is represented by me spinning in centre stage with my frock coat billowing out. When the spinning stops Scrooge is almost breathless with excitement (fortunately, for me, for I am too!), but notices that the Ghost's movements are tired, heavy and slow, and his voice a little breathless.

The ghost takes up a position at the front of the stage, in the very centre, to reveal the two pathetic, helpless characters of Ignorance and Want. In my early years of performing I didn't include this scene in my show as it is disturbing and has a nightmarish quality and I wasn't confident to bring the tone of the performance down – in my mind everything had to be entertaining and raise a laugh. But as my story-telling confidence grew I realised that this is a vital moment in the narrative and had to be witnessed.

To reveal the two children I plunge my hands deep

beneath my coat, as if untangling them, and I have occasionally wondered if there is some theatrical trick that I can use to make the moment even more shocking – maybe release a false flap of lining material which reveals a ghostly image beneath, or utilising some sort of puppetry to show the frailty of human life, but for now I have to rely on the imagination of the audience to give the skeletal creatures their form. In order to show off their frailty and to suggest the size of the giant, I hold my hands as if each hand is laid on the top of their heads, at a much lower level than a child would really be. I also send them off into their uncertain futures with the merest flick of a hand.

When Scrooge asks the ghost if they have no refuge or resource, he knows the answer and he is penitent as the reply comes in the form of his own words: 'Are there no prisons? Are there no workhouses' This last line I deliver as the ghost is disappearing into the air, so the last word is almost a final weak breath, becoming even more inaudible as I turn away from the audience leaving a black shape at the back of the stage. A slow tolling of a heavy church bell adds to the sombre tone of the scene, but when the figure turns it is not the next ghost, but Scrooge looking 'all about him for the Ghost of Christmas Present' I turn again, and let my right arm become the clapper striking the bell, holding it still until the final tone drifts away, giving a little flourish of my hand as an orchestra's conductor might do to bring a piece to an end.

Stave Four. The Last of the Spirits
The entrance of the Ghost of Christmas Yet to Come is a slow walk from the back of the stage to the front, and I try to capture an essence of floating rather than physical walking, as if this spirit has no recognisable realm to exist in, and on the line, '…leaving nothing of it visible save one outstretched hand' I

raise my right arm, with finger pointing to my side. I have already mentioned earlier in this book the workshop session back with the Design Theatre Workshop group when I was a teenager, and the sheer strength of the skeletal hand gesture is exhausting. Every muscle from my fingers, through my wrist, up my fore and upper arm is solid, rigid, straining, trembling, and in that moment my entire focus is concentrated on my fingers. You will notice that I use the word fingers, in the plural, and that is an important aspect to the look. My index is pointing forward, but my thumb is at ninety degrees to it to the side. My middle finger is forward, slightly beneath the line of the index, and then curled at the knuckle so the tip is pointing to the floor. The ring finger points directly down, whilst the little finger is up, horizontal on the same plane as the thumb and index finger. It is a powerful gesture and can be made even more effective if a stage light casts a shadow of the hand onto the back of the stage.

In the face of this powerful force, Scrooge falls to his knees and says 'I am in the presence of the Ghost of Christmas Yet to Come?' As I say the first part of the line I look all about me, as if the presence is all encompassing and filling the entire air, rather than being a single physical being, and when Scrooge asks for confirmation as to the spirit's identity, I hesitate through the line, as if he is trying to mentally come to terms with what he is actually saying: 'I am in the presence of... the ghost... of Christmas...' he looks back up to where the spirit is standing, '...yet to come?'

The arm comes back up and the finger points onward. Scrooge knows that he has no choice but to follow and from his penitent position on the floor he reaches his hand up to be lead into the future. Again, it is a strong gesture of the hand, but less skeletal, more human.

The first vision of the future is in no way nightmarish; indeed it is completely ordinary, featuring a trio of businessmen chatting in the street. To establish the scene, I position the ghost in the far upstage left corner of the stage, pointing on to where the conversation is taking place in the downstage right corner. The direction of the pointing here is important, for throughout the Ghost of the future is always pointing to the same spot - it is where Marley's grave was situated at the opening,

The Ghost of Christmas Yet to Come
Photo Credit: Phil Hinton

it is where Bob Cratchit gestures when taking about Tim's grave, and it will be the scene where Scrooge is shown the vision of his own grave. The Ghost of Christmas Yet to Come is always pointing towards death. The figure of Scrooge links the two, creeping from the ghost towards the gentlemen. The three are discussing the death of an acquaintance in a very matter of fact manner, and I distinguish between the three by voice and stance. The first voice is a bustling, busy man, confident and a little brash, the second has more natural class and doesn't try so hard, his observations are brief and to the point. The second is slightly shorter than the first, so when each talks his eyes are looking to where the other's face would naturally be. The third is much taller than both, standing with a slightly hunched stance, leaning on an imaginary walking cane, his voice is slightly husky. Again, the relative eyelines of each character helps to establish who is talking, as I make sure I look up, or down focussing on the position of the other two gents.

The scene passes insignificantly, as it does in the book and the old gents go their different ways. Scrooge looks about for his own image, and on the line, 'but although it was his usual time of day for being there, another man stood in his accustomed corner,' I look to the point where Scrooge had taken his melancholy dinner in his melancholy tavern. At that time he had sat on 'Bob Cratchit's stool', which has now vanished, in the same way that the character of Ebenezer has vanished from the London streets.

From the imagined bustling scene of the City of London the action moves to the shop owned by Old Joe. I play Joe as a vile caricature, an obscene monster, and as I recite the description of him, I let my face contort, and my body becomes sinuous as if he has many arms reaching out to grope whoever comes into his circle. This is a revolting character borne out of revolting language. As the description goes on, I drag my forearm across my nose making a sickening sniffing sound at the same time and by the time I am standing staring at an imaginary stalactite of slimy green mucus, the audience are hopefully squirming uncomfortably in their seats.

Sometimes if I am close to the front row of the audience, or in a dinner setting, I will select someone in the front row to wipe my hand clean on, which raises an even greater cry of 'Oh! Gross.' Now of course this scene is all played for comic effect, but it is also in the script because it reflects the language from the original text which, equally, makes the reader squirm:

'They left the busy scene, and went into an obscure part of the town, where Scrooge had never penetrated before,

195

although he recognised its situation, and its bad repute. The ways were foul and narrow; the shops and houses wretched; the people half-naked, drunken, slipshod, ugly. Alleys and archways, like so many cesspools, disgorged their offences of smell, and dirt, and life, upon the straggling streets and the whole quarter reeked with crime, with filth, and misery.

'Far in this den of infamous resort, there was a low-browed, beetling shop, below a pent-house roof, where iron, old rags, bottles, bones, and greasy offal, were bought. Upon the floor within, were piled up heaps of rusty keys, nails, chains, hinges, files, scales, weights, and refuse iron of all kinds. Secrets that few would like to scrutinise were bred and hidden in mountains of unseemly rags, masses of corrupted fat, and sepulchres of bones. Sitting in among the wares he dealt in, by a charcoal stove, made of old bricks, was a grey-haired rascal, nearly seventy years of age; who had screened himself from the cold air without, by a frousy curtaining of miscellaneous tatters, hung upon a line and smoked his pipe in all the luxury of calm retirement.'

It is another example of using a simple movement or gesture to recite whole paragraphs of narrative description. Charles Dickens wrote so vividly that his text comes alive on stage and screen, which is one reason that his works are continually adapted (that, and there being no copyright payable on his works anymore!). Incidentally, another influence in my portrayal of Old Joe is the spidery version of the character from the Muppets *Christmas Carol*.

In the book there are three visitors to the shop: the laundress, the charwoman and the undertaker, but I (and Dickens in his reading script) let them merge into the single character of Mrs Dilber, who I play as being worse for the influence of gin, her movements are unsteady and her voice slightly slurred. Once more I use a difference of height to bring some further interest to the scene, with Joe crouching on the floor to open the bundle of clothes, while Mrs Dilber looks on from above.

Old Joe
Photo Credit: Ian Dickens

The scene ends with Mrs D walking away, carelessly and unemotionally stating that she had removed the fine shirt from the corpse (we believe it to be that of Scrooge, although that is not confirmed at this point), before he was buried. The movement takes me upstage left towards the previous position of the ghost, meaning that I can transform into Scrooge again as I walk. At this point Scrooge is conversational with the ghost, as he had been with Past and Present, discussing what he has been shown and still assuming that all of the visions are for his education. As he mulls over what he has seen ('The case of this unhappy man might be my own, my life tends that way now'), he ambles backwards until his demeanour changes as suddenly a new vision has flashed before him. I make sure that I am now next to the chair which has also represented Scrooge's bed and as he sees it he recoils in horror. The narrative describes a bare bed, with no curtains around it which have obviously been removed by Mrs Dilber. Ebenezer is horrified at this constant squalid vision of death and now pleads for the ghost to show him a scene of tenderness, and for the first time since they entered the city, the ghost moves, leading Scrooge. The book states that 'The Ghost conducted him through several streets familiar to his feet' but I have slightly altered the line to say 'The Ghost led Scrooge through the streets he had already trodden with the Ghost of Christmas Present to: Bob Cratchit's dwelling.' By using these terms I can point towards the side of the audience first selected to be the Cratchit family in the Christmas dinner scene (stage left), and then swing the arm to the right and make my way slowly across the stage using ponderous steps. When I have reached the other side, I point out into the audience again, bowing my head slowly as I do so, until the figure is that of a statue on a tomb. All of the movements are designed to create a sense of loss, of mourning, of tragedy.

A question I am often asked is 'what is your favourite line in the show?' and the answer comes next: 'It was quiet. Very quiet.' If I have done everything right, if I have manipulated and convinced the audience effectively, then there will be absolute silence at this moment, and I can hold the pause between the two parts of the line for a long time. More than applause and laughter and shouting, it is this moment that gives me the greatest thrill on stage. Naturally there will be days when the magic is broken by a mobile phone going off, or someone sneezing, but that is rare.

The following scene is a conversation between Bob and Mrs Cratchit, whose character I establish by gently wiping her hands on her 'apron', as I did when she first appeared. In Mrs C's first scene she was a figure of comedic fun but now she must be a genuine, empathetic, caring wife so I ensure that although her movements and voice are recognisable, there is no hint of foolishness about her. She asks Bob if he had been to the cemetery, and in an effort to control his emotions, he delays his answer by removing his coat and carefully hanging it on the coat rack. There was a time when I would carefully make sure that the sleeves were pulled inside out during this moment, but more of that later. Having hung his coat Bob turns back to his wife, holding his hands up, as if gently holding hers.

This is a scene that I have changed over the last few years to reflect Dickens' original intentions more accurately. For many years I suggested that Bob had actually been visiting Tim's grave, telling his wife how green a place it is, and that they would visit often. As he spoke, he gently picked up the abandoned cane (representing the simple crutch), as if that was the only way that he could hold his son again, and remembering him, broke down clutching the cane to him. But the actual truth of the scene is that Bob has visited the site of the grave where Tim will be buried, for the body is still in the upstairs bedroom. In the new version Bob Cratchit picks up the cane, holding it close, as before, but now as he falters he runs from the room, leaving Mrs Cratchit behind, and upstairs. I do this by imagining a door to the right of the stage, then turning right into an imaginary hall, then right again onto the stairs, which lead directly to the bedroom door. This circuitous move takes me back into the same space that I have just been performing in but now we believe that it is another room. He walks towards the little table where the folded cloth, that I had prepared back in the Fezziwig scene and placed in its current position when Bob had carried Tim home on his shoulder, is laid upon it, with the single candle in the simple candlestick behind it. The Tiny Tim tableau is now a shrine. Bob sits on the stool next to the table and after a moment to gather his thoughts and emotions, he leans over to kiss his son. Dickens tells us that Bob 'was reconciled to what had happened, and went down quite happy.'

He leaves the room, down the imaginary staircase, enters the downstairs room, hands held out to hold his wife and other children, but as I walk, I transform into Scrooge walking towards the Ghost of Christmas Yet to Come who is still in his position in the upstage left corner of the stage. Now he must face the question 'what man that was whom we saw lying dead?' It is in this moment that everything he has witnessed, from the image of his old school, his separation from Belle, the dismissiveness of the businessmen in the street, to the inevitable tragedy of the Cratchit family, focuses into the final vision. When Scrooge asks the ghost, I say the words as if he really knows the answer but must face the reality.

The Spirit points on and walks to the centre of the stage where he stops and drops his finger, pointing down to a stone laid on the grass: this is another recreation of the original John Leech illustration.

From its position at the centre of the stage the ghost then turns, still facing the stone and moves away backwards towards the chair/bed. Scrooge is left scrabbling on the floor pleading and promising that he will 'honour Christmas in my heart and try to keep it all the year. I shall live in the Past, the

Present and the Future, the spirits of all three shall strive within me.' As he mentions the three ghosts, he gestures to the spot that the first spirit appeared by the bed, then out into the auditorium where the second stood to tell him that Tiny Tim would die, and finally to the position that the dark spectre has taken up by the bed. He holds up his hands, pleading to be given another chance but instead witnesses the ghost collapsing before his eyes. The fear of Scrooge now is that this is the inevitability of death, and he has now completed his journey to the grave, and there is no chance to change his life, or the lives of those around him. He clutches at the ghost crying out 'don't leave me here, please don't leave me here!' (Another addition of mine, these lines do not feature in the original), and looking up finds himself kneeling by his own bed clinging tightly to the bed post.

Stave 5: The End of It.

From this moment on the atmosphere lifts and it is joyfulness to the end. Scrooge gradually becomes aware of his surroundings, and clutches hold of the imaginary bed curtains which have not been torn down by Mrs Dilber. His movements around his room are rapid as the realisation dawns on him that the bed is his own, the room is his own and, best and happiest of all, the time before him is his own to make amends in, but it is important to remember that he is still physically the same old man who we met just a few hours before – his bones, joints and muscles have not been rejuvenated overnight, so I must make sure that those frailties are still apparent. One way of doing this is when he drops to his knees, calling out to the ghost of Jacob Marley 'Heaven and the Christmas time be praised for this. I say it on my knees old Jacob, on my knees!' when he tries to rise to his feet again it is a bit of an effort, requiring the assistance of his hand.

His sense of joy is completely youthful, however, and the skipping around the stage calling out to all and sundry is a tribute to one of the happiest scenes in cinema: Alastair Sim in his nightshirt from the 1951 film version of *A Christmas Carol.*

Next, he runs to the window and flings it open to be greeted by a loud peal of church bells (one of the few sound effects in my show), and this recreates the narrative passage, 'He was checked in his transports by the churches ringing out the lustiest peals he had ever heard. Clash, clang, hammer; ding, dong, bell. Bell, dong, ding; hammer, clang, clash! Oh, glorious, glorious!'

The 'window' is situated downstage centre (rather confusingly in exactly the same spot that the room door was, when Jacob Marley's ghost entered, but I offer my artistic licence as defence), and Scrooge is looking down on the streets below where he catches sight of a young boy – I imagine the same one who was signing carols the night before. The child has a cockney chirrup to his voice, and a slight mocking tone as if it is a good sport to tease the old miser. When the boy shouts 'Christmas Day!' in answer to Scrooge's question 'What's today my good fellow?' the old man is confused, for in his mind he has been with the spirits through three days – the first ghost appeared at midnight and spent an entire day showing visions of the past. The second also came in the night and stayed for twelve hours before handing over to the Ghost of Christmas Yet to Come. How could today still be Christmas day? And then the reality dawns upon him and I let a look of comprehension and delight take over my face as he looks to the heavens: 'The spirits have done it all in one night...' I remember that it was this moment that had the greatest effect in me when I first heard the story as a five-year-old. Scrooge's delight at talking with the boy is evident and he giggles to himself 'An intelligent boy! A remarkable boy.' And 'What a delightful boy! It's a pleasure to talk to him!' The distance between them is created by height, Ebeneezer looking down and to his right as if from an upstairs window, whilst the boy is craning his neck to look up to the left.

Having sent the boy to fetch the prize turkey, Scrooge has a fit of the giggles as he tells us his plan to anonymously send the bird to the Cratchit family. This laughter is born from Charles Dickens' words: 'Really, for a man who had been out of practice for so many years, it was a splendid laugh, a most illustrious laugh. The father of a long, long line of brilliant laughs!'

He runs to the coat rack to retrieve the coat placed there by the mournful Bob Cratchit, and tries to put it on, but in his excitement he can't, it whirls about him until he throws it onto the floor in desperation.

Photo Credit: Ian Dickens

The coat scene is one that has grown-up in recent years, mainly thanks to Liz's observations and suggestions, and the show is better (and shorter) for it. There were days, in my more insecure past, when only laughter mattered – mirth was the barometer of success, and at this point of the show I literally threw any sense of scene or character away in the pursuit of happiness. If you remember, when Bob Cratchit had removed the coat, I mentioned that I would turn the sleeves inside out, unseen by the audience, and carefully hang it up? Well, now of course Scrooge could not get his coat on, and in his frustration would fling it not onto the floor, but far into the auditorium. The scene continues until the moment that Ebenezer prepared to 'get dressed all in his best', and leave his apartment, of course his best – his coat – was nowhere to be seen, and it would suddenly dawn upon me that I had flung it away. I would shuffle awkwardly to the front of the stage and gesture to whoever had the coat (they would often gleefully hold it up to show me that they held it), the coat would be passed to the front where I could reach down and gently drag it onto the stage, at which time I would hiss 'it's OK, I don't think anyone noticed…' The show would appear to be back on track, until I discovered that the sleeves were turned inside out, which of course I had done earlier. I would then hold up the coat by the sleeve, look to whoever had retrieved it and say, 'Thanks a lot!' I would pull a sleeve the right way in, before discovering that the other one was reversed too, leading to my berating continuing, 'Oh, both of them!' I would then angrily put my coat on and continue with the story. As you can tell from this description, the whole business was distracting and very long winded and destroyed any sense of continuity to Charles Dickens' story. Apart from that it turned a wonderfully joyful moment into a confrontational one. However odd it seems to me now, I kept that scene in for years and years because people loved it and laughed. When I eventually removed this silly bit of business a few years ago my signing lines were full of people saying 'But, oh! We missed the coat!' It was, however, the correct decision and one I should have taken long ago.

Now the scene flows much more quickly, but there is still a little bit of tomfoolery to the moment. Scrooge grabs his coat and puts it on without pause, then grabs his top hat, and flings it up in the air spinning over and over, the idea being that it lands squarely on his head as he walks to the door. Of course, it very rarely does and just bounces onto the floor. I pick it up, place it jauntily onto my head saying cheerfully, 'One day! One day!' and walk into the next scene. On the very few (maybe once a season) occasions that the hat does land on my head there is inevitably a huge cheer, and I am completely confused as how to continue!

As I leave Scrooge's room, I grab the cane which is resting against Tiny Tim's stool and then pause for a moment to practice saying 'Merry Christmas', for Ebenezer hasn't uttered those words for many years. As he strides into the street he is continually muttering 'Merry Christmas' under his breath and his concentration is such that he almost collides with a passer-by, he snaps around and growls 'get out of my way!' before walking on and continuing his sotto voce repetition of 'Merry Christmas!' And then he realises what he has done, this was his first opportunity to present a new face to the world and he has failed. I stop, turn to look after the poor pedestrian who has just been shouted out (who, of course, wouldn't have thought twice about being berated by Ebenezer Scrooge), and run after him, holding out a hand to stop him in his path. An apology is offered and reiterated, and then I mime holding out my hand to shake his, saying quietly and genuinely 'a Merry Christmas'. I pause with my hand outstretched and then very slowly move it up and down as if the invisible stranger has indeed decided to respond to the offer. From being a tentative shake at first, the handshake becomes vigorous and hearty. This I see as another very important moment in the story, for it is proof to Ebenezer that a simple kind gesture brings a return. Buoyed by his newfound knowledge old Scrooge makes his way down the street shaking everyone's hands, greeting them, and bidding them all a Merry Christmas, even kissing the hand of a lady and wishing her 'Enchanté mademoiselle!' None of these passers-by have words, or any physical response, but I have a strong vision in mind as to how each looks and sounds.

Among the bustling streets Scrooge then catches sight of the charity collector whom he had sent packing the night before, and rushes up to him. The conversation between the two men features a little piece of theatrical trickery that I am rather proud of. When Scrooge first addresses the man he takes his hat off, holding it and his walking cane in his right hand. When the charity collector replies I transfer the hat to my left hand, keeping the cane in his right, and when Scrooge speaks again, the hat is passed back to the right, meaning that each character looks different to the audience, even if they can't quite work out why that is. When the gentleman drops his hat and cane in the shock of hearing what Mr Scrooge wishes to donate, it is Ebenezer who bends down to retrieve them, and he brushes the dust of a London street off before handing them back. This insignificant action is as a result of a drama workshop session back when I was in my teens, I had been asked to mime a car mechanic carrying out a repair and as I stood up, I absentmindedly mimed wiping the spanner clean. The leader of the workshop immediately chimed in by saying to the group 'Look! We now know that this is a careful and conscientious mechanic because he keeps his tools in good condition all the time, instead of just throwing them into his greasy toolbox.' A simple, apparently insignificant action can speak so much, and Scrooge's careful brushing of the hat and cane tells the audience a great deal about his new state of mind.

The line 'Scrooge went to church' is played in different ways for different audiences and venues. If, for instance, I am actually in a church performing for a mainly congregational audience, I will linger over the moment, maybe even walking slowly up the isle of the sanctuary until I can kneel before the altar. At the little Ebenezer Chapel in Occoquan, of course, I could use my well-rehearsed 'they even named it after me' ad-lib.

On stage I will simply mime the opening of a large heavy door and removing my hat as I bow my head in reverence. From Church I place my hat at a jaunty angle (making sure that I have mimed leaving through the door again), and stride to nephew Fred's house, and when I rush up to knock at the door use my cane to knock on the wooden stool: 'rat tat ta tat!' My current cane is made from a hard wood and leaves little indentations on the stool (at new venues I have to be sure to ask that it is OK to knock on their furniture in this way), so that you can always tell how many times I have performed: count the marks and divide by five.

Of course, Scrooge is welcomed in to the house with open arms, 'Wonderful party, wonderful games, won-der-ful happiness!', after the word 'games' I put in Topper's 'Helll-oooo' to briefly recreate the earlier Blindman's buff scene.

The show could stop here, but there is one more scene to be played out. The final pose of the party scene is me standing at the centre of the stage with my arms spread wide, but slowly they drop to my side, I hunch my shoulders and begin walking: Scrooge is returning to his office on the next morning. I mime flinging the door open and grab Cratchit's stool, placing it near to the front of the stage in the very centre. I take off the top hat and place it, along with the cane, on the hatstand, but keeping the scarf on. I pull my pocket watch out as I continue the narrative, 'The clock struck nine. No Bob!' The 'No' being a particularly long version of the word, and 'Bob' being clipped in such a way that it is the final consonant that does all of the work. I pace to the other side of the stage, 'The clock struck a quarter past nine. Noooooo…' and here I pause, as if I have either forgotten, or am unable to say, the word, and hopefully the audience will complete the line for me: 'BOB!', to which I cheerfully reply 'Thank you very much!'

I transform into Bob Cratchit who is rushing into the office, knowing he is late, with his scarf flowing out behind him, he unwraps it and flings it towards the hatstand where, hopefully, it lands and hangs next to the top hat that is already there. He plumps himself on his stool and begins to write, as if he has been seated there for hours. I take a pose with a very straight back, taken from the final illustration of *A Christmas Carol*.

In the voice of Scrooge I bark 'What do you mean by coming here at this time of day,' and Cratchit is back to being the nervous, stuttering character, rather than the more kindly, confident man we have seen in his own household. Eventually Scrooge tells Bob to come into his office, and the words he uses are important, for he says, 'Step this way if you please… Cratchit!' In the opening scene of the show he never uses anybody's names, so the fact he does now hints at the change that has come over him despite the gruff and challenging demeanour.

As he teases his clerk, he prods him and pushes him back towards the stool, where he forces him down as he announces that he has decided to 'raise your salary!' For this moment I remain in the physical character of Ebenezer, standing behind the stool with my hands as if on Cratchit's shoulders pushing him down, but on the word 'salary' I step forward and sit on the stool and am now the astonished Bob, eyes and mouth wide open, again in the straight-backed pose. I pause for a moment, and then leap from the stool grab it, and brandish it towards Scrooge as an old-fashioned circus lion tamer may have done. This movement is inspired from the passage in the book where Dickens suggests that Cratchit considered calling into the street for a straight jacket to be brought, assuming that the old man is in fact insane. But after a short while Cratchit replaces the stool on the exact spot that it was in, and his facial expression tells the audience that he has seen something in Scrooge's eyes that convince him of his sincerity. In placing the stool down I can extend the movement to take me back to Ebenezer's position on the stage and I continue the scene as him. His delight and generosity are unmistakable. As he talks, he fetches his hat and cane from the stand, meaning that when he tells Bob that 'I shall endeavour to assist your struggling family' he holds up the cane, representing Tiny Tim's crutch.

Having insisted that Cratchit goes and buys a new coalscuttle (I find this an interesting choice, for it shows that Ebenezer is still the businessman, and wants Cratchit's workplace to be more comfortable. He also promises to discuss his affairs that very afternoon, but he doesn't decide to give poor Bob the rest of the day off!), I am left 'alone' on the stage, and I stand behind the stool to deliver the final passages of narrative. On delivering the last line, 'God Bless Us, Every One', I conclude by wishing the audience a very merry Christmas and leave the stage, leaving them in no doubt that it is now time to clap, cheer and stamp!

Chapter 10
The Script of A Christmas Carol

This is the script of my two-act version of *A Christmas Carol* as I performed it during 2022 Christmas season. It has been adapted over the years from Charles Dickens' original reading script. Although the bones of the show have remained unchanged since I first performed in 1993, I am constantly looking for ways to change or improve it, often adding particular passages from the original book that I am fond of. Other changes are apparent in the way I have staged and presented the show:

A Christmas Carol

HOUSE LIGHTS DOWN, COOL LIGHTING ON STAGE

THE FIRST MUSIC CUE PLAYS (THE OPENING BARS OF THE TRANS SIBERIAN ORCHESTRA'S SARAJEVO/CHRISTMAS EVE, FOLLOWED BY THE TOLLING OF A DEEP CHURCH BELL. IT STRIKES FOUR TIMES).

GERALD ENTERS AS SCROOGE WALKING BEHIND JACOB MARLEY'S COFFIN. AS THE FIRST CHURCH BELL TOLLS HE LOOKS ROUND SHARPLY AND

REMOVES HIS TOP HAT. AT THE THIRD BELL TOLL HE SCOFFS AND TURNS AWAY. AFTER THE FOURTH HE LOOKS AT THE AUDIENCE.

Marley was dead: to begin with. There is no doubt whatever about that. The register of his burial was signed by the clergyman, the clerk, the undertaker, and the chief mourner.

Scrooge signed it. And Scrooge's name was good upon 'Change, for anything he chose to put his hand to. Old Marley was as dead as a door–nail.

Mind! I don't mean to say that I know what there is particularly dead about a door–nail. Do you? I might have been inclined, myself, to regard a coffin–nail as the deadest piece of ironmongery in the trade, would you agree? Good, because it is in the book! But the wisdom of our ancestors is in the simile; and my unhallowed hands shall not be allowed to disturb it, or the Country's done for.

So, you will therefore permit me to repeat, emphatically, that Marley was as dead as… **HE ENCOURAGES THE AUDIENCE TO JOIN IN WITH THE END OF THE LINE** a door–nail.

Scrooge knew he was dead? Of course he did. How could it be otherwise? Scrooge and he were partners for I don't know how many years.

Scrooge was his sole executor, his sole administrator, his sole assign, his sole residuary legatee, his sole friend, and sole mourner.

And even Scrooge was not so dreadfully cut up by the sad event, but that he was an excellent man of business on the very day of the funeral, and solemnised it with an undoubted bargain.

The mention of Marley's funeral brings me back to the point I started from. There is no doubt that Marley was dead. This must be distinctly understood, or nothing wonderful can come of the story I am going to relate.

Scrooge never painted out Old Marley's name. There it stood, years afterwards, above the warehouse door: Scrooge and Marley.

The firm was known as Scrooge and Marley. Sometimes people new to the business called Scrooge 'Scrooge', and sometimes Marley, but he answered to both names. It was all the same to him.

Oh! But he was a tight–fisted hand at the grind–stone, Scrooge! a squeezing, wrenching, grasping, scraping, clutching, covetous, old sinner! Hard and sharp as flint, secret, and self–contained, and solitary as an oyster.

The cold within him froze his old features, nipped his pointed nose, shrivelled his cheek, stiffened his gait; made his eyes red, his thin lips blue; and spoke out shrewdly in his grating voice.

External heat and cold had little influence on Scrooge. No warmth could warm, no wintry weather chill him. Nobody ever stopped him in the street to say, with gladsome looks, 'My dear Scrooge, how are you? Even the blind men's dogs appeared to know him; and when they saw him coming on, would tug their owners into doorways and up courts.

But what did Scrooge care! It was the very thing he liked. To edge his way along the crowded paths of life, warning all human sympathy to keep its distance.

HE MOVES AS IF ENTERING THE OFFICE AND THE LIGHTS BECOME BRIGHTER AND HE SITS IN THE CHAIR

Once upon a time—of all the good days in the year, on Christmas Eve—old Scrooge sat busy in his counting–house. It was cold, bleak, biting weather: foggy withal:

The city clocks had only just gone three, but it was quite dark already— it had not been light all day—and candles were flaring in the windows of the neighbouring offices, like ruddy smears upon the palpable brown air. and even though the court was of the narrowest, the houses opposite were mere phantoms.

The door of Scrooge's office was open that he might keep his eye upon his clerk, who in a dismal little cell beyond, a sort of tank, was copying letters. Scrooge had a very small fire, but the clerk's fire was so very much smaller that it looked like one coal. But he couldn't replenish it, for Scrooge kept the coal–box in his own room; and so surely as the clerk came in with the shovel, the master predicted that it would be necessary for them to part company.

Wherefore the clerk put on his comforter and tried to warm himself at the candle; in which effort, not being a man of a strong imagination, he failed.

FROM STAGE LEFT GERALD HAS NOW BECOME FRED. HE UNBUTTONS THE FROCKCOAT AND RUSHES INTO THE SCENE

'A merry Christmas, uncle! God save you!' cried the cheerful voice of Scrooge's nephew, who came upon him so quickly that this was the first intimation he had of his approach.

'Bah!' said Scrooge, 'Humbug!'

FRED CARELESSLY UNRAVELS HIS SCARF AND THROWS IT ONTO THE CHAIR

'Christmas a humbug, uncle!' said Scrooge's nephew. 'You don't mean that, I am sure?'

'I do, If I could work my will, every idiot who goes about with "Merry Christmas" on his lips, should be boiled with his own pudding, and buried with a stake of holly through his heart. He should!'

'Uncle!'

'Nephew!' 'Keep Christmas in your own way, and let me keep it in mine.'

'Keep it! but you don't keep it.'

'Let me leave it alone, then,' said Scrooge. 'Much good may it do you! Much good it has ever done you!'

'Uncle I have always thought of Christmas time, when it has come round—apart from the veneration due to its sacred name and origin, if anything belonging to it can be apart from that—as a good time; a kind, forgiving, charitable, pleasant time: And therefore, uncle, though it has never put a scrap of gold or silver in my pocket, I believe that it has done me good, and will do me good; and I say, God bless it!'

The clerk in the Tank involuntarily applauded.

CRATCHIT CLAPS LOUDLY BUT FREEZES, TURNING TO WHERE SCROOGE IS STANDING, THE APPLAUSE PETERING OUT PATHETICALLY

Becoming immediately sensible of the impropriety, he poked the fire, and extinguished the last frail spark for ever.

'Let me hear another sound from you,' said Scrooge, 'and you'll keep your Christmas by losing your situation! You're quite a powerful speaker, sir, I wonder you don't go into Parliament.'

'Don't be angry, uncle. Come! Dine with us tomorrow.'

Scrooge said that he would see him—yes, indeed he did. He went the whole length of the expression, and said that he would see him in that extremity first!

'The nephew left the room without an angry word,

notwithstanding. As he left he bestowed the season's greetings upon the clerk, who cold as he was, was warmer than Scrooge for he returned them cordially.

In letting the nephew out so the clerk let another gentleman in – a portly gentlemen, pleasant to behold, who now stood in Scrooge's office with books and papers in his hand.

'Scrooge and Marley's, I believe, do I have the pleasure of addressing Mr Scrooge, or Mr Marley?'

'Mr Marley has been dead these seven years. He died seven years ago, this very night. What do you want?'

'Oh! I'm sorry, I have no doubt his liberality is well represented by his surviving partner.'

'At this festive season of the year, Mr Scrooge, it is more than usually desirable that we should make some slight provision for the Poor and Destitute, who suffer greatly at the present time. Many thousands are in want of common necessaries; hundreds of thousands are in want of common comforts, sir.'

'Are there no prisons?'

'Plenty of prisons.'

And the Union Workhouses are they still in operation?

'They are. Mr Scrooge, I wish I could say that they were not, but under the impression that they scarcely furnish Christian cheer of mind or body 'a few of us are endeavouring to raise a fund to buy the Poor some meat and drink, and means of warmth. We choose this time, because it is a time, of all others, when want is keenly felt, and abundance rejoices. What shall I put you down for?'

'Nothing!'

'Oh! I see you wish to remain anonymous?'

'I wish to be left alone.'

HE MOVES STAGE LEFT AND MIMES OPENING THE DOOR, THEN RETURNS TO HIS DESK WHERE HE STARTS TO WORK'

'Since you ask me what I wish, sir, that is my answer. I don't make merry myself at Christmas and I can't afford to make idle people merry. I help to support the establishments I have mentioned—they cost enough; and those who are badly off must go there.'

'Many can't go there; and many would rather die.'

'If they would rather die, then they had better do it, and decrease the surplus population. Good afternoon, gentlemen!'

Seeing clearly that it would be useless to pursue his point, the gentleman withdrew.

Foggier yet, and colder! Piercing, searching, biting cold. The owner of one scant young nose, gnawed and mumbled by the hungry cold as bones are gnawed by dogs, stooped down at

Scrooge's keyhole to regale him with a Christmas carol: but at the first sound of 'God bless you, merry gentlemen! May nothing you dismay!'

Scrooge seized the ruler with such energy of action, that the singer fled in terror, leaving the keyhole to the fog and even more congenial frost.

At length the hour of shutting up the counting–house arrived.

SCROOGE LOOKS AT HIS WATCH AND THEN COMMANDS CRATCHIT TO STAND BEFORE HIM.

'You! Here! You'll want all day to–morrow, I suppose?'

'If quite convenient, sir.'

'It's not convenient, and it's not fair. If I was to stop you half–a–crown for it, you'd think yourself ill–used, I'll be bound? And yet, you don't think me ill–used, when I pay a day's wages for no work.'

'It is only once a year, sir!'

'A poor excuse for picking a man's pocket every twenty–fifth of December!' 'But I suppose you must have the whole day. Be here all the earlier next morning.'

The clerk promised that he would; and pelted home to Camden Town to play at blindman's–buff.

'There's another fellow, my clerk, speaking of a merry Christmas. I should retire to Bedlam!'

Scrooge shut up the office and made his way into the city streets.

SCROOGE OPENS THE DOOR WALKS INTO THE STREET. AS HE WALKS HE BARKS AT A PASSERBY: 'GET OUT OF MY WAY!'

He took his usual melancholy dinner in his usual melancholy tavern; and having read all the newspapers, and beguiled the rest of the evening with his banker's–book, went home to bed.

Now, it is a fact, that there was nothing at all particular about the knocker on Scrooge's door, except that it was very large. It is also a fact, that Scrooge had seen it, night and morning, during his whole residence in that place; also that Scrooge had as little of what is called fancy about him as any man in the city of London.

But, as he had his hand upon the lock, he saw in the knocker, not a knocker but Marley's face!

SNAP WHITE SPECIAL ON MARLEYS FACE

Marley's face with a dismal light about it, like a bad lobster in a dark cellar. It was not angry or ferocious, but looked at Scrooge as Marley used to look: with ghostly spectacles turned up on its ghostly forehead.

As Scrooge looked fixedly at this phenomenon, it was a knocker again.

SPECIAL OUT

To say that he was not startled, or that his blood was not conscious of a terrible sensation to which it had been a stranger from infancy, would be untrue. But he put his hand upon the key he had relinquished, turned it sturdily, walked in, and lighted his candle.

He did pause, with a moment's irresolution, before he shut the door; and he did look cautiously behind it first, as if he half-expected to be terrified with the sight of Marley's pigtail sticking out into the hall. But there was nothing on the back of the door, except the screws and nuts that held the knocker on, so he said 'Pooh!' And went upstairs: trimming his candle as he went for it was very dark.

Up Scrooge went, not caring a button for that. Darkness is cheap, and Scrooge liked it.

But before he shut his heavy door, he walked through his rooms to see that all was right. He had just enough recollection of the face to desire to do that.

Sitting–room, bedroom, lumber–room. All as they should be. Nobody under the Chair, nobody under the table; nobody in his dressing–gown, which was hanging up in a suspicious attitude against the wall.

Quite satisfied, he locked his door, double-locked his door, which was not his custom, and sat down .

As he threw his head back in the chair, his glance happened to rest upon a bell, a disused bell, and as he watched it slowly began to swing. soon it rang out loudly, and so did every bell in the house. They stopped, as they had begun, together.

They were succeeded by a clanking noise, deep down below; as if some person were dragging a heavy chain over the casks in the wine merchant's cellar below. The cellar–door flew open with a booming sound, and then he heard the noise much louder, on the floors below; then coming up the stairs; then coming straight towards his door. 'It's humbug still! I won't believe it.'

It came on through the heavy door, and passed into the room before his eyes. Marley's Ghost!'

LIGHTING EVEN COOLER

The same face: the very same. Marley in his pigtail, usual waistcoat, tights and Boots. The chain he drew was clasped about his middle. It was long, and wound about him like a tail; and it was made of cash-boxes, keys, padlocks, ledgers, deeds, and heavy purses wrought in steel.

His body was transparent; so that Scrooge looking through him could see the two buttons on his coat behind.

Scrooge had often heard it said that Marley had no bowels, but he had never believed it until now.

'How now!' said Scrooge, caustic and cold as ever. 'What do you want with me?'

'Much!'—Marley's voice, no doubt about it

'Who are you?'

'Ask me who I was.'

'Who were you then?'

'In life I was your partner, Jacob Marley.'

'Can you — can you sit down?'

'I can.'

'Do it, then.'

'You don't believe in me, what evidence would you have of my reality beyond that of your senses? Why do you doubt your senses?'

'Because, a little thing affects them. A slight disorder of the stomach makes them cheats. You may be an undigested bit of beef, a blot of mustard, a crumb of cheese, a fragment of an underdone potato. There's more of gravy than of grave about you, whatever you are!'

MARLEY CRIES OUT, SENDING SCROOGE TUMBLING BACK INTO HIS CHAIR

'Mercy! Dreadful apparition, why do you trouble me? Why do spirits walk the earth, and why do they come to me?'

'It is required of every man that the spirit within him should walk abroad among his fellow men, and travel far and wide; and if that spirit goes not forth in life, it is condemned to do so after death and witness what it cannot share, but might have shared on earth, and turned to happiness!'

'You are fettered, Tell me why?'

'I wear the chain I forged in life, I made it link by link, and yard by yard; I girded it on of my own free will, and of my own free will I wore it. Is its pattern strange to you? Or would you know the weight and length of the strong coil you bear yourself? It was full and as heavy and as long as this, seven Christmas Eves ago. You have laboured on it, since. It is a ponderous chain !'

'Jacob, Old Jacob Marley, tell me more. Speak comfort to me, Jacob!'

'I have none to give, A very little more, is all permitted to me. I cannot rest, I cannot stay, I cannot linger anywhere. My spirit never walked beyond our counting-house — mark me!— in life my spirit never roved beyond the narrow limits of our money-changing hole; and weary journeys lie before me! 'Hear me! My time is nearly gone.'

'I am here to–night to warn you, that you may have yet a chance and hope of escaping my fate. A chance and hope of my procuring, Ebenezer.'

'You will be haunted, by Three Spirits.'

'Is that the chance and hope you mentioned, Jacob?'

'It is.'

'Then I think I'd rather not!'

'Without their visits you cannot hope to shun the path I tread. Expect the first tomorrow, when the bell tolls One.' 'Expect the second on the next night at the same hour. The third upon the next night when the last stroke of Twelve has ceased to vibrate. Look to see me no more.'

When it had said these words, the spirit walked towards the window and floated into the bleak, dark, night.

LIGHTS BACK TO PREVIOUS COOL

Scrooge tried to say 'Humbug!' but stopped at the first syllable. And being, from the emotion he had undergone, or the fatigues of the day, or the dull conversation of the Ghost, or the lateness of the hour, much in need of repose; went straight to bed, without undressing (obviously!), and fell asleep upon the instant.

HE SLEEPS. LIGHTS DIM BUT NOT TO FULL BLACKOUT

Scrooge awoke as the church clock Tolled a deep, dull, hollow, melancholy ONE.

LIGHTS SNAP UP. COOL

The curtains of his bed were drawn aside, and Scrooge, found himself face to face with the unearthly visitor who drew them:

It was a strange figure—like a child: yet not so like a child as like an old man, viewed through some supernatural medium, which gave him the appearance of having receded from the view, and being diminished to a child's proportions.

'Are you the Spirit, sir, whose coming was foretold to me?' asked Scrooge.

'I am.'

'Who, and what are you?' Scrooge demanded.

'I am the Ghost of Christmas Past.'

'Long Past?' inquired Scrooge.

'No. Your past. The things that we shall see are but shadows of the things that have been,' said the Ghost. 'They have no consciousness of us. Rise, and walk with me.'

As the words were spoken, they passed through the wall, and stood upon an open country road, with snow upon the ground.

LIGHTS UP BRIGHT MORNING

'Good Heaven! I was bred in this place. I was a boy here.'

'You recollect the way?'

'Remember it? I could walk it blindfold.'

'Strange to have forgotten it for so many years, let us go on.'

They walked along the road, Scrooge recognising every gate, and post, and tree; until a little market–town appeared in the distance, with its bridge, its church, and winding river. Some shaggy ponies now were seen trotting towards them with boys upon their backs, who called to other boys in country gigs and carts, driven by farmers. All these boys were in great spirits, and shouted to each other.

The jocund travellers came on; and as they came, Scrooge knew and named them everyone. Why was he rejoiced beyond all bounds to see them? Why did his cold eye glisten, and his heart leap up as they went past? Why was he filled with gladness when he heard them give each other Merry Christmas, as they parted at cross-roads and bye-ways, for their several homes? What was merry Christmas to Scrooge? Out upon merry Christmas! What good had it ever done to him?

'The school. It is not quite deserted. A solitary child, neglected by his friends, is left there still.'

BACK TO COOL STATE

They went across the hall, to a door at the back of the house. It opened before them, and disclosed a long, bare, melancholy room. A lonely boy was reading near a feeble fire; and Scrooge sat down upon a form and wept to see his poor forgotten self as he used to be.

Poor boy! Poor boy, 'I wish but it's too late now.'

'What is the matter?' asked the Spirit.

'Nothing,' said Scrooge. 'Nothing. There was a boy singing a Christmas Carol at my door last night. I should like to have given him something: that's all.'

The Ghost smiled thoughtfully.

'Let us see another Christmas.'

Scrooge's former self grew larger at the words, and the room became a little darker and more dirty. The panels shrunk, the windows cracked; fragments of plaster fell out of the ceiling, and the naked laths were shown instead; but how all this was brought about, Scrooge knew no more than you do. He only knew that it was quite correct; that everything had happened so; that there he was, alone again, when all the other boys had gone home for the jolly holidays.

He was not reading now but walking up and down despairingly.

Scrooge looked at the Ghost, and with a mournful shaking of his head, glanced anxiously towards the door.

It opened; and a little girl, much younger than the boy, came darting in, and putting her arms about his neck, and often kissing him, addressed him as her, 'Dear, dear brother!'

'I have come to bring you home, dear brother!' 'To bring you home, home, home! You are never to come back here; and we're to be together all the Christmas long, and have the merriest time in all the world!'

227

'You are quite a woman, little Fan!'

Always a delicate creature, whom a breath might have withered, but she had a large heart.'

'So she had.'

'She died a woman,' and had, as I think, children.'

'One child. My nephew. Fred.'

Although they had but that moment left the school behind them, they were now in the busy thoroughfares of a city.

The Ghost stopped at a certain warehouse door, and asked Scrooge if he knew it.

'Know it? I was apprenticed here!'

They went in.

LIGHTS WARM

At sight of an old gentleman in a Welsh wig, sitting behind such a high desk, that if he had been two inches taller he must have knocked his head against the ceiling, Scrooge cried in great excitement:

'Why, it's old Fezziwig! Bless his heart; it's Fezziwig alive again.'

'Yo ho, there! Ebenezer! Dick!'

Scrooge's former self, came briskly in, accompanied by his fellow–prentice.

'Dick Wilkins, to be sure! Bless me, yes. There he is. He was very much attached to me, was Dick. Poor Dick. Dear, dear.'

'Yo ho, my boys. No more work to–night! Christmas Eve, Dick. Christmas, Ebenezer. Let's have this place cleared away, before a man can say Jack Robinson.'

DURING THE FOLLOWING THE STOOL GETS MOVED FROM DOWNSTAGE TO UPSTAGE, AND THE SCARF GETS HUNG UP ON THE HAT STAND.

Clear away? There was nothing they wouldn't have cleared away, or couldn't have cleared away, with old Fezziwig looking on and the warehouse was as snug, and warm, and dry, and bright a ball–room, as you would desire to see upon a winter's night.

UP ONTO THE CHAIR AND SCREEECHES LIKE A VIOLIN TUNING

In came a fiddler and went up to the lofty desk, and made an orchestra of it, and tuned like fifty stomach–aches. In came Mrs Fezziwig, one vast substantial smile. In came the three Miss Fezziwigs, beaming and lovable. In came the six young followers whose hearts they broke.'

There were dances, and there were forfeits, and more dances, and there was cake, there was a great piece of Cold Roast, and there was a great piece of Cold Boiled, and there were mince–pies, and plenty of beer.

But the great effect of the evening came after the Roast and Boiled, when the fiddler struck up 'Sir Roger de Coverley.'

MUSIC CUE TWO: SFX SIR ROGER DE COVERLEY

Then old Fezziwig stood out to dance with Mrs Fezziwig. Top couple, too; with a good stiff piece of work cut out for them; three or four and twenty pair of partners; people who were not to be trifled with; people who would dance, and had no notion of walking.

But if they had been twice as many—ah, four times— old Fezziwig would have been a match for them, and so would Mrs Fezziwig. As to her, she was worthy to be his partner in every sense of the term.

SFX FADE

When the clock struck eleven, this domestic ball broke up.

BACK TO COOL TWO AS MR FEZZIWIG IS SEEN SHAKING HANDS WITH THE GUESTS AS THE SCENE FADES

Scrooge felt the Spirit's glance, and stopped.

'What is the matter?'

'Nothing in particular.'

'Something, I think.'

'Oh, very well. I should like to be able to say a word or two to my clerk… Bob… Cratchit. That's all.'

'My time grows short.'

Again Scrooge saw himself. He was older now; a man in the prime of life and he sat by the side of a fair young girl in whose eyes there were tears.

'Another idol has displaced me Ebenezer;

'What Idol has displaced you?'

'A golden one.'

SHE PULLS AN IMAGINARY ENGAGEMENT RING FROM HER FINGER AND THROWS IT TOWARDS SCROOGE AND RUNS FROM HIM.

'Belle, come back here, don't go away . Come back!

AS OLD SCROOGE, IN HORROR CALLING TO HIS FORMER SELF

'Go after her man, don't let her go… don't… let… her go…'

'Spirit, show me no more.'

'One shadow more.'

They were in another scene and place; a room, filled with the tumultuous activity of a large and boisterous family. Near to the fire sat a beautiful young girl, so like that last that Scrooge believed it was the same, until he saw her, now a comely matron, sitting opposite her daughter. and when he thought that such another creature, quite as graceful and as full of promise, might have called him father, and been a spring–time in the winter of his life, his sight grew very dim indeed.

'Belle,' said the husband, 'I saw an old friend of yours this afternoon.'

'Who was it?'

'Guess!'

'I don't know!'

'Guess!'

'Oh, you know I don't like games! I don't know! Oh, I'm all of a flutter! Not Mr Scrooge?'

'Mr Scrooge it was. I passed his office window; and as it was not shut up, and he had a candle inside, I could scarcely help seeing him. His partner, Jacob Marley, lies upon the point of death, I hear; and there he sat, old Ebenezer, alone. Quite alone in the world, I do believe.'

'Spirit! Show me no more! Haunt me no longer!'

And as Scrooge struggled with the spirit he was conscious of being exhausted, and, further, of being in his own bedroom. and had barely time to reel to bed, before he sank into a heavy sleep.

Blackout. Interval

Act Two

CUE THREE: VOICEOVER IN BLACKOUT

You will be haunted by Three Spirits. Expect the first tomorrow, when the bell tolls One. Expect the second on the next night at the same hour.

LIGHTS UP COOL

Awaking in the middle of a prodigiously tough snore, and sitting up in bed to get his thoughts together, Scrooge had no occasion to be told that the bell was again upon the stroke of One.

Now, being prepared for almost anything, he was not by any means prepared for nothing; and, consequently, when the Bell struck One, and no shape appeared, he was taken with a violent fit of trembling. Five minutes, ten minutes, a quarter of an hour went by, yet nothing came. All this time, he lay upon his bed, the very core and centre of a blaze of ruddy light.

He began to think that the source and secret of this ghostly light might be in the adjoining room, from whence it seemed to shine. He got up softly and shuffled in his slippers to the door.

STRONG WARM LIGHT UP

The moment Scrooge's hand was on the lock, a strange voice called him by his name, and bade him enter.

'Come in! Come in and know me better man!'

It was his own room. There was no doubt about that. But it had undergone a surprising transformation. The walls and ceiling were so hung with living green, that it looked a perfect grove.

Heaped up on the floor, to form a kind of throne, were turkeys, geese, game, poultry, brawn, great joints of meat, sucking–pigs, long wreaths of sausages, mince–pies, plum–puddings, barrels of oysters, red–hot chestnuts, cherry–cheeked apples, juicy oranges, luscious pears, immense twelfth–cakes, and seething bowls of punch, that made the chamber dim with their delicious steam.

In easy state upon this throne, there sat a jolly Giant, glorious to see, who bore a glowing torch, and held it up, high up, to shed its light on Scrooge, as he came peeping round the door.

'Come in!' exclaimed the Ghost. 'Come in, and know me better, man. I am the Ghost of Christmas Present. Look upon me.'

It was clothed in a green robe, and this garment hung so loosely on the figure, that its capacious breast was bare. Its hair was long and free; free as its genial face, its sparkling eye, its open hand, its cheery voice, its unconstrained demeanour, and its joyful air.

'You have never seen the like of me before?'

'No! Never, 'Spirit, I went forth last night on compulsion, and I learnt a lesson which is working now. To–night, if you have aught to teach me, let me profit by it.'

'Touch my robe.'

Scrooge did as he was told, and held it fast.

Holly, mistletoe, red berries, ivy, turkeys, geese, game, poultry, brawn, meat, pigs, sausages, oysters, pies, puddings, fruit, and punch, all vanished instantly. So did the room, the fire, the hour of night, and they stood in the city streets on Christmas morning.

The people were all so eager and hurried that sometimes they tumbled up against one another but when there were angry words between them, the ghost shed a few drops of water on them from his torch and their good humour was restored directly. For they said, 'It's a shame to quarrel upon Christmas Day!' And so it was. God love it, so it was.

'The Spirit led Scrooge through the streets to…Here?' To Bob Cratchit's dwelling and there the Ghost of Christmas Present blessed his four–roomed house.

Then up rose Mrs Cratchit,

'What has ever got your precious father then? And your brother, Tiny Tim they weren't as late last Christmas Day by half–an–hour.'

And as the words were spoken, in came little Bob, with Tiny Tim upon his shoulder. Alas for Tiny Tim, he bore a little crutch, and had his limbs supported by an iron frame.

GERALD GRABS ROLLED RED CLOTH AND SITS IT ON HIS SHOULDER TO REPRESENT TINY TIM. HE ALSO GETS THE WALKING CANE TO BE THE CRUTCH.

The two young Cratchits hustled Tiny Tim, and bore him off into the wash-house, that he might hear the pudding singing in the copper. **LAYS CLOTH ON USTAGE TABLE AND CANE ON THE STOOL.**

'And how did little Tim behave?' asked Mrs Cratchit.

'As good as gold, and better. Somehow he gets thoughtful, sitting by himself so much, and thinks the strangest things you ever heard. He told me, coming home, that he hoped the people saw him in the church, because he was a cripple, and it might be pleasant to them to remember upon Christmas Day, who made lame beggars walk, and blind men see. He is growing strong and hearty.'

Back came Tiny Tim before another word was spoken, escorted by his brother and sister to his stool before the fire.

Mrs Cratchit made the gravy hissing hot; Master Peter mashed the potatoes with incredible vigour; Miss Belinda sweetened up the apple–sauce.

At last the cloth was laid and grace was said. It was succeeded by a breathless pause, as Mrs Cratchit, looking slowly all along the carving–knife, prepared to plunge it in the breast; but when she did, and when the long-expected gush of stuffing issued forth, one murmur of delight arose around the table.

GERALD WAITS FOR A RESPONSE FROM THE AUDIENCE TO STAGE LEFT AND WHEN NONE IS FORTHCOMING, SIGHS:

'You do a one man show and they expect you to do all of the work yourself!'

HE WALKS TO STAGE RIGHT AND REPEATS THE LINE

'One murmur of delight arose around the table!'

THE WHOLE AUDIENCE WILL GASP AND HE BERATES THE STAGE LEFT SIDE

'It's too late now! I'm going to take my goose over here now!'

HE CARRIES AM IMAGINARY PLATTER ACROSS THE STAGE AND FROM NOW ON THE STAGE RIGHT AUDIENCE REPRESENT THE CRATCHITS

There never was such a goose. Bob said he didn't believe there ever was such a goose cooked. Eked out by the apple–sauce and mashed potatoes, it was a sufficient dinner for the whole family.

But now, Mrs Cratchit left the room alone—too nervous to bear witnesses—to take the pudding up and bring it in.

Supposin' Supposin' it should not be done enough? Supposin' Supposin' it should break in turning out? Supposin' Supposin' somebody should have got over the wall of the back-yard, and stolen it?

Hallo! A great deal of steam. The pudding was out of the copper. A smell like a washing–day! That was the cloth. A smell like an eating–house and a pastrycook's next door to each other, with a laundress's next door to that! That was the pudding. In half a minute Mrs Cratchit entered—flushed, but smiling proudly—with the pudding, like a speckled cannon–ball, blazing with ignited brandy.

Oh, a wonderful pudding.

ENCOURAGING THE AUDIENCE TO GASP ONCE MORE

Well remembered!

Bob Cratchit said, and calmly too, that he regarded it as the greatest success achieved by Mrs Cratchit since their marriage. When all was done Bob stood and proposed.

'A Merry Christmas to us all, my dears! God bless us!'

'God bless us every one!' said Tiny Tim

'Spirit,' said Scrooge, with an interest he had never felt before, 'tell me if Tiny Tim will live.'

'I see a vacant seat in the poor chimney–corner, and a crutch without an owner, carefully preserved.'

'No, no, say he will be spared!'

'If these shadows remain unaltered by the Future, the child will die. What then? If he be like to die, he had better do it, and decrease the surplus population.'

Scrooge hung his head to hear his own words used against him.

It was a great surprise to Scrooge to hear a hearty laugh. It was a much greater surprise to Scrooge to recognise it as his own nephew's.

'He said that Christmas was a humbug, as I live! He believed it too!'

'More shame for him, Fred,' said Scrooge's niece by marriage.

'Oh I am sorry for him; I couldn't be angry with him if I tried. Who suffers by his ill whims? Himself, always. Here, he takes it into his head to dislike us, and he won't come and dine with us. What's the consequence? He don't lose much of a dinner!'

'Indeed, I think he loses a very good dinner.'

'Well, I'm very glad to hear it, because I haven't great faith in these young housekeepers. What do you say, Topper?'

Topper had clearly got his eye upon one of Scrooge's niece's sisters, for he answered that a bachelor was a wretched outcast, who had no right to express an opinion on the subject either way. Whereat Scrooge's niece's sister—the plump one with the lace tucker—blushed.

After a while they played at forfeits; for it is good to be children sometimes, and never better than at Christmas, when its mighty founder was a child himself.

Stop! There was first a game at blind–man's buff. Of course there was. And I no more believe Topper was really blind than I believe he had eyes in his boots. The way he went after that niece's sister was an insult, an outrage.

Wherever she went, so went he. If you had fallen up against him (as some of them did), in an effort to be caught, he would have made a feint of endeavouring to seize you, which would have been an affront to your understanding, and would instantly have sidled off in the direction of the niece's sister.

She often cried out that it wasn't fair; and it really was not, and No doubt she told him her opinion of it, when, another blind–man being in office, they were so very confidential together, behind the curtains.

The whole scene passed off in the instant and again Scrooge and the sprit where upon their travels.

DURING FOLLOWING, LIGHT GRADUALLY DIM TOWARDS COOL

Much they saw, and far they went, and many homes they

visited, but always with a happy end. The Spirit stood beside sick beds, and they were cheerful; on foreign lands, and they were close at home; by poverty, and it was rich.

And when they stood together in an open space, Scrooge noticed that the Sprit's hair was grey.

'Are spirits' lives so short?'

'My life upon this globe is very brief, it ends to–night.'

'To–night!'

'To–night at midnight.

CUE FOUR: SFX, A CLOCK STRIKING THE THREE QUARTER.

Hark! The time is drawing near.'

From the foldings of its robe, it brought forth two children; wretched, abject, frightful, hideous, miserable. Scrooge startled back in terror.

'Spirit, are they yours?'

'They are Man's, and they cling to me. This boy is Ignorance. This girl is Want. Beware them both, and all of their degree, but most of all beware this boy, for on his brow I see that written which is Doom.

'Have they no refuge or resource?'

'Are there no prisons?' Are there no workhouses?'

CUE FIVE. SFX BELL TOLLING MIDNIGHT.

The clock struck twelve.

LIGHTS V COLD NOW.

Scrooge looked about him for the Ghost of Christmas Present, and saw it not. As the last stroke ceased to vibrate, he remembered the prediction of old Jacob Marley, and lifting up his eyes, beheld a solemn Phantom, draped and hooded, coming, like a mist along the ground, towards him.

It was shrouded in a deep black garment, which concealed its head, its face, its form, and left nothing of it visible save one outstretched hand.

'I am in the presence of the Ghost of Christmas Yet to Come?'

The Spirit answered not but pointed onward with its hand.

'Ghost of the Future!' he exclaimed, 'I fear you more than any spectre I have seen. But as I know your purpose is to do me good, and as I hope to live to be another man from what I was, I am prepared to bear you company. Lead on, Spirit, Lead on.'

They scarcely seemed to enter the city; for the city rather seemed to spring up about them, but there they were, in the heart of it; The Spirit stopped beside one little knot of business men. Observing that the hand was pointed to them, Scrooge advanced to listen to their talk.

MOVES DSR AND BECOMES 3 GENTLEMEN TALKING

1: 'No,' said a great fat man with a monstrous chin, 'I don't know much about it, either way. I only know he's dead.'

2: 'When did he die?' inquired another.

1: 'Last night, I believe.'

3: 'What has he done with his money?' Asked a third.

1: 'I haven't heard, left it to his company I expect, he hasn't left it to me. That's all I know.'

3: 'It's likely to be a very cheap funeral, upon my word I can't think of anyone to go to it. Suppose we make up a party and volunteer?'

2: 'Oh yes, I'll go, of course I shall go. If lunch is provided, I must be fed! Well, farewell, toodlepip!'

RETURNS TO USL WHERE GHOST IS

Scrooge was surprised that the Sprit should attach importance to a conversation apparently so trivial.

He looked about in that very place for his own image; but another man stood in his accustomed corner, and though the clock pointed to his usual time of day for being there, he saw no likeness of himself among the multitudes.

They left the busy scene, and went into an obscure part of the town, to a low–browed, beetling shop, where iron, old rags, bottles, bones, and greasy offal, were bought by a grey–haired rascal, of great age.

An old woman with a heavy bundle slunk into the shop.

'What odds then? What odds, who's the worse for the loss of a few things like these? Not a dead man, I suppose!' open that bundle, old Joe, and let me know the value of it.

Old Joe went down on his knees and opened the bundle:

'What do you call this? 'Bed–curtains?'

'Bed–curtains!'

'You don't mean to say you took them down, rings and all, with him lying there?'

'Yes I do. Ah! you may look through that shirt till your eyes ache; but you won't find a hole in it, nor a threadbare place. It's the best he had. They'd have wasted it if it hadn't been for me.'

'What do you call wasting of it?'

'Putting it on him to be buried in, to be sure.' 'Somebody was fool enough to do it, but I took it off again.'

'Spirit, I see, I see. The case of this unhappy man might be my own. My life tends that way, now. Merciful Heaven, what is this?'

He recoiled in terror, for the scene had changed, and now he almost touched a bed: a bare, uncurtained bed: on which, beneath a ragged sheet, there lay a something covered up, which, though it was dumb, announced itself in awful language.

'Let me see some tenderness connected with a death, or that dark chamber, Spirit, which we left just now, will be for ever present to me.'

GHOST LEADS SCROOGE FIRST TO DSL, THEN ACROSS STAGE TO DSR WHERE HE POINTS OUT TO THE AUDIENCE REPRESENTING THE CRATCHIT FAMILY

The Ghost led Scrooge through the streets he had trodden with the Ghost of Christmas Present to: Bob Cratchit's dwelling.

Quiet. Very quiet.

Little Bob came in. Alone.

Mrs Cratchit hurried out to meet him. 'You went today, then, Robert?'

'Yes, my dear. I wish you could have gone. It would have done you good to see how green a place it is. But you'll see it often. I promised him that we would walk there on a Sunday. Oh! My little, little child. My little child.'

He broke down all at once. He couldn't help it. If he could have helped it, he and his child would have been farther apart perhaps than they were.

He left the room, and went up-stairs to the room above, it was cheerfully lit and hung with Christmas. There was a chair set close beside the child, Poor Bob sat down in it, and he kissed the little face. He was reconciled to what had happened, and went down again quite happy.

Spectre, something informs me that our parting moment is at hand. I know it, but I know not how. Tell me what man that was whom we saw lying dead.

GHOST POINTS TO THE GRAVE DSR, WHERE MARLEY'S WAS

The spirit led Scrooge to A churchyard. And pointed down to the grave by which they stood. Here then Scrooge was to learn the name of the man who had lain upon that bed.

'Before I draw nearer to that stone to which you point, tell me, are these the shadows of the things that will be, or are they shadows of things that may be, only?'

The Spirit was immovable as ever.

Scrooge crept towards it, trembling as he went; and following the finger, read upon the stone his own name, Ebenezer Scrooge.

'No, Spirit. Oh no, no!' I am not the man I was! I will not be the man I must have been but for this! Why show me this, if I am past all hope?'

The kind hand trembled.

'I will honour Christmas in my heart, and try to keep it all the year. I will live in the Past, the Present, and the Future. The Spirits of all Three shall strive within me. I will not shut out the lessons that they teach. Oh, tell me I may sponge away the writing on this stone!'

In his agony, he caught the spectral hand. The Spirit, stronger yet, repulsed him.

Holding up his hands in a last prayer to have his fate reversed, he saw an alteration in the Phantom's hood and dress. It shrunk, collapsed, and dwindled down.

It dwindled down into…

LIGHTS TO WARM

… a bedpost!

Yes! and the bedpost was his own. The bed was his own, the room was his own. Best and happiest of all, the Time before him was his own, to make amends in!

'I will live in the Past, the Present, and the Future. The Spirits of all Three shall strive within me. Oh, Jacob Marley, Heaven, and the Christmas Time be praised for this. I say it on my knees, old Jacob, on my knees.'

His hands were busy with his garments all this time; turning them inside out, putting them on upside down, tearing them, mislaying them.

TRIES TO PUT HIS COAT ON BUT CAN'T, SO THROWS IT TO THE FLOOR

'I don't know what to do! I am as light as a feather, I am as happy as an angel, I am as merry as a schoolboy! I am as giddy as a drunken man! A merry Christmas to everybody! A happy New Year to all the world! Hallo here! Whoop! Hallo!'
He ran to the window, and opened it.

CUE SIX: SFX PEALING OF MORNING CHURCH BELLS
No fog, no mist; clear, bright, shining Golden sunlight.

'What's today?' cried Scrooge, calling downward to a boy who was passing.

'Eh?

SFX: FADES

'What's today, my fine fellow?'

'Today? Why, Christmas Day!'

'It's Christmas Day! I haven't missed it! The Spirits have done it all in one night. They can do anything they like. Of course they can. Of course they can. Hallo, my fine fellow!'

'Hallo!'

'Do you know the Poulterer's, in the next street but one, at the corner?' Scrooge inquired.

'I should hope I did,' replied the lad.

'An intelligent boy! A remarkable boy. Do you know whether they've sold the prize Turkey that was hanging up there—Not the little prize Turkey; the big one?'

'What, the one as big as me?'

'What a delightful boy! It's a pleasure to talk to him. Yes, my buck!'

'It's hanging there now.'

'Is it! Go and buy it! and tell the man to bring it here, that I may give him the direction where to take it. Come back with him in less than five minutes and I'll give you half a crown!

'I'll send it to Bob Cratchit's.' 'He shan't know who sent it. It's twice the size of Tiny Tim.'

He dressed himself all in his best, and at last got out into the streets.

PICKS COAT UP, PUTS IT ON, GRABS HAT FROM THE STAND AND SPINS IT INTO THE AIR, TO LAND ON HIS HEAD

He had not gone far, when coming on towards him he beheld the portly gentleman, who had walked into his counting–house the day before, and said, 'Scrooge and Marley's, I believe.'

'My dear sir, how do you do? I hope you succeeded yesterday. It was very kind of you. A merry Christmas to you, sir.'

'Mr Scrooge?'

'Yes. That is my name, and I fear it may not be pleasant to your ears. Allow me to ask your pardon. And will you have the goodness'—here Scrooge whispered in his ear.

'Lord bless me! My dear Mr Scrooge, are you serious?'

Deadly! 'Not a penny less. A great many back–payments are included in it, I assure you. Will you do me that favour?'

'My dear sir, I don't know what to say to such munif…'

'Don't say a word, please, just come and see me at my office tomorrow. Will you come and see me?'

'I will! Mr Scrooge, I will. A Merry Christmas to you. God Bless You!'

'And a merry Christmas to you too, and God bless you… Oh! My word…'

SCROOGE SEARCHES FOR THE CHURCH AND GOES IN.

He went to church, and walked about the streets, and watched the people hurrying to and fro, and patted children on the head, questioned beggars, looked down into the kitchens of houses, and up to the windows, and found that everything could yield him pleasure. In the afternoon, he turned his steps towards his nephew's house.

He passed the door a dozen times before he had the courage to go up and knock. But he made a dash, and did it.

'Why bless my soul! Who's that?'

'It's I. Your uncle Scrooge. I have come to dinner. Will you let me in, Fred?'

Let him in! It is a mercy he didn't shake his arm off! He was at home in five minutes. Wonderful party, wonderful games, wonderful unanimity, won-der-ful happiness.

But.

TAKES THE FORM OF OLD SCROOGE AS HE WALKS TO HIS OFFICE DOOR

He was early at the office next morning. Oh, he was early there. If he could only be there first, and catch Bob Cratchit coming late. That was the thing he had set his heart upon.

And he did it; yes, he did. The clock struck nine. No Bob. A quarter past. No Bob. He was full eighteen minutes and a half behind his time.

His hat was off, before he opened the door; his comforter too. He was on his stool in a jiffy; driving away with his pen, as if he were trying to overtake nine o'clock.

'Hallo! What do you mean by coming here at this time of day?'

'I am very sorry, sir, I think I am behind my time.'

'You are? Yes. I think you are.'

'It's only once a year Mr Scrooge. We were making rather merry yesterday, sir.'

'Step this way, sir, if you please, Cratchit.'

'Now, I'll tell you what my friend, I am not going to stand this sort of thing any longer. And therefore,' he continued, 'giving Bob such a dig in the waistcoat that he staggered back into the Tank again and therefore I am about to raise your salary.'

'Eh?'

'A merry Christmas, Bob. 'A merrier Christmas, Bob, my good fellow, than I have given you for many a year! I'll raise your salary, and endeavour to assist your struggling family, and we will discuss your affairs this very afternoon, over a Christmas bowl of smoking bishop, Bob. Make up the fires, and buy another coal–scuttle before you dot another I, Bob Cratchit.'

SPECIAL REDUCING TO A SINGLE SPOT DOWNSTAGE CENTRE

Scrooge was better than his word. He did it all, and infinitely more and to Tiny Tim, who did not die, he was a second father. He became as good a friend, as good a master, and as good a man, as the good old city knew, or any other good old city, town, or borough, in the good old world. Some people laughed to see the alteration in him, but he let them laugh, and little heeded them. His own heart laughed and that was quite enough for him.

It was always said of Scrooge, that he knew how to keep Christmas well, if any man alive possessed the knowledge. May that be truly said of us, and all of us! And so, as Tiny Tim observed, God bless us, Everyone!

Have a very Merry Christmas!

BLACKOUT

BOWS

THE END

CUE SEVEN SFX DECK THE HALLS WITH BOUGHS OF HOLLY AS AUDIENCE LEAVE

God Bless Us, Every One!
Photo Credit: Phil Hinton